"The genius of Jeffrey Bays' book is that it takes something remarkably simple, something most writers and filmmakers take for granted — the scene transition — and elevates it to an art form. *Between the Scenes* may not teach you how to be a storyteller, but take it to heart and it'll teach you how to set yourself apart from all the other storytellers out there."

— Chad Gervich, TV writer: *Dog with a Blog*, *After Lately*, *Cupcake Wars*; Author: *How to Manage Your Agent*; *Small Screen, Big Picture*

"*Between the Scenes* takes all the guessing out of scene transitions. It explains the magic behind sequencing and dissects our favorite films that do this the best. This book helps make everyone that reads it a better storyteller by focusing on this key fundamental tool as the reader will start recognizing the opportunities to connect their story emotionally with their audience."

— Libby Blood, Associate Editor, *SVN Student Filmmaking*

"Illuminating and essential for viewing, making, and exploring all aspects of film. We think of transitions as editing. Bays shows you all the forces at work that make an enriching, complete film."

— Dave Watson, Editor, *Movies Matter*

"Scene transitions help any script, film ████ one scene to the next — leading the ████ wondrous journey. *Between the Scen*████ script or film from a good one to a g.████

— Matthew Terry, writer, teacher, reviewer for *www.microfilmmaker.com*

"For novice or pro — or even the committed film buff — *Between the Scenes* is a reminder of the extraordinary power of film language and the profound impact of rightly placed images, sounds, and metaphors — the very punctuation — that give energy, meaning, and life to the narrative. This wonderful volume will help any storyteller to become more proficient in his craft. Highest recommendation."

— Robin E. Simmons, filmmaker and screenwriter, movie columnist at the *CV Weekly*, *CoachellaValleyWeekly.com*

"*Between the Scenes,* the first book to deal solely with the art of cinematic transitions, helps first-time filmmakers to anticipate this specific type of creative choice and to make it correctly. Whether writing, directing, or editing, you'll find this is a practical text devoted to helping you strengthen the impact of your film by eliciting the right emotional connection from your audience."

— Greg Marcks, director of *11:14* and *Echelon Conspiracy*

"Being a producer, I read many scripts. Scene transitions are often omitted, misused, or overlooked completely. *Between the Scenes* is a thorough roadmap to proper, more powerful scene transitioning. An important tool for student and professional screenwriters alike. Thank you, Michael."

— Rod Hamilton, producer, *Dirty Love*,
Who the F Is Buddy Applebaum

"*Between the Scenes* is a must-have book for anyone who is serious about making great films. It is full of ideas and inspiration! The fresh, practical approach breaks down how and why transitions are so important to storytelling by analyzing hundreds of films in a user-friendly way. It cuts out the film school mumbo-jumbo and shows anyone who writes, directs, or edits how they can use transitions to take their film to the next level."

— Theresa Villeneuve, Professor of Film, Citrus College

"Jeffrey Michael Bays new book provides the reader filmmaker with much needed 'food for thought' for making one's story and movie that much better. Read it, learn and benefit from the suggestions he makes. His approach helps you be a much more thoughtful and thorough storyteller and that makes it worth the read."

— Rex Sikes Movie Beat

"*Between the Scenes* serves as an exhaustive how-to book for how filmmakers can approach transitional and interstitial moments between scenes. Focusing on specific approaches that writers, directors, and editors can each take to navigate transitions, Bays' book will be a welcome addition to many filmmakers' bookshelves."

— David Tarleton, Head of Editing and Post-Production,
Columbia College, Chicago

"*Between the Scenes* is the 'missing link' of film directing books! Jeffrey takes us on a well researched journey to prove why scene transitions are the best kept secret of storytelling — because they help us connect our stories emotionally with the audience. If you want to be a better filmmaker, this book is a MUST read!"

— Peter D. Marshall, director, film directing coach

BETWEEN THE
SCENES

What Every Film Director, Writer, and Editor Should Know About Scene Transitions JEFFREY MICHAEL BAYS

Published by Michael Wiese Productions
12400 Ventura Blvd., # 1111
Studio City, CA 91604
tel. 818.379.8799
fax 818.986.3408
mw@mwp.com
www.mwp.com

Cover design by Johnny Brenner www.johnnyink.com
Interior layout by Gina Mansfield Design
Copyedited by David Wright

Printed by McNaughton & Gunn, Inc., Saline, Michigan
Manufactured in the United States of America

Library of Congress Cataloging-in-Publication Data

Bays, Jeffrey Michael, 1977-
Between the scenes : what every film director, writer, and editor should know
about scene transitions / Jeffrey Michael Bays.
    pages cm
  ISBN 978-1-61593-169-9 (pbk.)
1. Motion pictures--Production and direction. I. Title.
  PN1995.9.P7B3243 2014
  791.4302'32--dc23
                                2013033458

Printed on recycled stock.
Publisher plants ten trees for every one tree used to produce this book.

FSC
www.fsc.org
MIX
Paper from
responsible sources
FSC® C011935

In Memory of my Grandma,
IRENE AUCUTT (1918 – 2011)

CONTENTS

The dates and directors of all films cited
in the text can be found in the Filmography.

ACKNOWLEDGMENTS

A number of people were invaluable in helping me complete this book.

I am indebted to my original thesis supervisor, Anna Dzenis, for giving me the courage to climb the mountain of research in the beginning. Thanks to Gabrielle Murray and all the Cinema Studies lecturers at La Trobe University who inspired me to think outside the box. I'd also like to thank the staff of the La Trobe library — especially Ross Schnioffsky, who was always helpful in finding the sources needed.

A special thank you to all of my good friends that took the time to proofread and suggest sources: Andrew Magee, Bailey Smith, Morgan McLeod, Foti Vrionis, Luke Zimbler, and Eleanor Colla. And a heartfelt thanks to William Shirriffs for making me laugh during the tough times.

Many thanks to Glenn Maxwell for providing the illustrations, and to Aikira Chan for the Gestalt giraffe drawing in Chapter 8.

Thanks to Corey Druskin for his script sample in Chapter 4.

This book would not have been possible without composer Spike Suradi, who introduced me to many great films during my time in Australia, provided encouragement, and was always available to discuss the theories of music scoring.

My love and thanks to my family for nourishing my passion for film and letting me set sail on this journey.

PERMISSIONS

INTRODUCTION

"Transitions are everything in movies.
They are the unsung hero."

— STEPHEN GAGHAN, screenwriter, director

How do film scenes fit together?

It wasn't until I got to the editing room that I realized just how much scene placement mattered. When you place blocks of scenes into a sequence in the editing timeline, rhythms and moods emerge that aren't inherently contained in each scene. Transitions between these scenes rise to your full attention, as they either make magic or fall flat. I had a sense of how it would all work, but one thing became clear — it never turns out the same as it does in your head.

The craft of scene transitions is the best kept secret of storytelling. Up until now it has been a hidden art form, relegated to the realm of instinct.

I'm not going to teach you how to edit, direct, or write a screenplay. There are other books for those things. In this book, I hope to make you a better storyteller. By focusing on the transition from one scene to the next, you'll start to see more clearly those opportunities to connect your story emotionally with your audience. You'll begin to see your scene transitions as a fertile ground to sow the seeds of story, to ripen the fruits of plot.

It's something that most of us never think of until it's too late. As filmmakers, we spend so much time worrying about rehearsing and blocking the actors, the set design, the dialogue, the shot selection — a frantic myriad of decisions that must be made quickly. At every stage of the game we tend to compartmentalize everything into scenes. We worry about things like: *Do we have all the props we need for Scene 36? What's Jane's backstory for Scene 24?*

When these individual scenes are all complete and placed next to each other in the editing timeline, suddenly they start to flow together. *Oops!* We really should have shot more footage of the house exterior. Suddenly it becomes clear that there is a bigger process at work here, rising above the compartmentalized scenes. Rhythms and emotions aren't working as well as we thought they would. The editing room then becomes a rescue center, the place to reshape and save the film.

Hopefully that doesn't sound familiar. It happened to me on my first film.

On many productions, the rhythm of placing scenes together is a combination of instinct and luck. The writers, directors, and editors feel it. If it feels right and looks right, it must be right, right?

A few years ago I set out to find if there's really a craft behind this magic. The surprising thing is — I couldn't find anything written about it. There was no book about the art of scene transitions.

That was pretty shocking because, after all, the place where the scenes join is where all the drama is. Everything happens there. It's where the characters change and move, it's where big plot revelations surface, and it's where the audience thinks. As screenwriter Stephen Gaghan once said, "transitions are everything in movies." I knew there was something to this, but I wasn't having any luck finding answers.

So I put my detective hat on and for two years made it my life's mission — to uncover this hidden art of scene transitions. I combed through academic textbooks, essays from the great film critics, and the classic *Art of Cinema* by Lev Kuleshov, a pioneering director and film theorist. So much massive attention has been spent on scene structure over the years, but very little has been written about how those scenes connect. Any mention of scene transitions was just a brief aside to some other topic, or a short checklist of possible match cuts.

I began to wonder why the topic had been so marginalized. Either it was just such common knowledge that nobody bothered to look at it in depth, or there's something deeper to it that no one could pinpoint. Clearly a lot of people were missing it, because one of the biggest embarrassments seen in student films, amateur productions, home movies (and yes, even some Hollywood blockbusters) is the lack of thought put into connecting scenes. I can't count the number of times I have been jarred out a story's world after a misplaced fade-to-black, or got bored with a lengthy action sequence because there were no ebbs and rhythms to balance the intensity.

As I watched and analyzed more movies by focusing entirely on their *scene transitions*, I began to see trends and commonalities in the great films. Techniques were being used and repeated throughout the decades. Aha, Watson! There really is a hidden art form here. New, exciting theories emerged from the research which I drew upon in composing my master's thesis. This book takes that research and those theories, and translates them into an easy-to-follow journey for filmmakers like you to add to your creative tool kit.

You and I are in the midst of a "gold rush" of filmmaking. More and more people are taking it up than ever before, in the hopes of finding a golden connection with an audience. The difference between amateur films that make you cringe and those that ignite your imagination with a compelling story is scene transitions. With a mastery of transitions, it will become easier for you to create the golden moments that touch people on a visceral level.

HOW TO USE THIS BOOK

This book is about style. It's about shaping the content that is already in your script. It's about adding and omitting content for the purposes of sharpening clarity or provoking questions. Most importantly, it's about how to translate those script pages into dramatic visuals that connect with the audience. It will prevent the "rescue center" mentality of the editing room and allow for comfortable and informed editing options.

You can turn to this book at every phase of production, from the early drafts of your script to the final touches in the editing room. Each chapter is written as a separate entity to help you dive into the book's middle and still understand it. If you have a specific concern in your current script, you'll be able to turn to that section and find what you need.

The simplest concepts are in the earlier chapters: choosing locations with boundaries, connecting the boundaries, moving your heroes through those boundaries. In later chapters, you'll find more about pacing and rhythmic concerns. Rather than this being just a catalog of transition techniques, you'll find an in-depth focus on the art behind transitional choices.

My hope is to make this book accessible to everyone, especially those who are currently immersed in a film project and looking for inspiration. I will use a mix of practical techniques along with some deeper science. It's important to know what makes these things tick so you're not just emulating the examples in this book, but can create your own ideas from proven principles.

LOOKING AT FILMS IN A NEW WAY

Right now you're probably thinking, "Transitions are just those little things that connect my scenes." By the end of this book you'll be thinking, "Scenes are just those little things that connect my transitions."

Digging into the content between the scenes is a new approach to the filmmaking craft. By focusing more attention on your transitions, you will open up a whole new realm of possibilities. Other books talk about scenes, structure, plot points, etc. You'll find that this book says little about what happens in your scenes. Instead, we look at what happens at the end of one scene and the beginning of the next. Naturally, this is where the dynamic changes happen in your story, so this is where our focus will be. You'll also explore how blocks of scenes fit together and how they interact.

You'll begin to think more about what happens off-screen between your scenes. Your decision of what to leave on screen and what to omit plays a crucial role in the emotional flow of your film.

FROM INSTINCT TO CRAFT

Up until now scene transitions have been created from instinct. It's something your director knows and doesn't have time to explain to you. Or, it's something your director doesn't really know consciously but instinctively uses it to guide her creative decisions. For a long time we assumed that scenes could just be thrown together with some match cuts and that was the only thought necessary. When it worked, nobody questioned it. When something didn't work — we just tried something until it felt right.

Let's pull up the hood and look at the inner workings of this instinctual engine. Screenwriting guru Robert McKee says *instinct* is "trial by error against a model built up from accumulated reading and watching." In other words, you make creative choices by comparing your film to all the films you've ever seen before. Or, you might have something echoing in your head from what a film instructor may have said in class.

True instinct is knowing first how the craft works and then making a gut/artistic judgment on whether it worked in this instance.

The art of filmmaking has only been around for a little more than a hundred years and transitions have been a part of it since the very beginning. Transitions were a natural progression when scenes began to be constructed. By the 1920s everyone had already figured out how to use dissolves, wipes, cuts, and all of the transitional styles that we use today.

There are reasons that some techniques have survived and others haven't. The craft of scene transitions does exist, and it's still evolving. For the first time, this book breaks down everything into its parts and explores the nuts and bolts of this craft. I've analyzed the art of scene transitions from nearly every possible angle and approach, boiling them down to the basics.

THE HIDDEN ART: WHY NOBODY NOTICES

Just like anything in filmmaking, if it's done right nobody notices. We are so accustomed to the shapes and shifts of scene changes that we don't even think about them. The scene transitions are when we are the most intimately connected with the characters and forget we are watching a movie. It is the moment when we have the most engagement, the most feelings, and the most thought.

As filmmakers, we do need to notice. The choices you make at this dramatic shift from one scene to another have a profound impact on your audience. At the end of the day, the art of scene transitions is about connecting with that audience. If you can do that, everyone is happy.

Now, let's get started!

CHAPTER ONE

WHAT IS A SCENE TRANSITION?

"When I'm making a film, I'm the audience."

— MARTIN SCORSESE, director

At a recent convention, I stepped into an elevator and found myself sharing the ride with Andrew Probert, the designer of the ships in *Star Trek: The Next Generation*, including the interiors of the *Enterprise D*.

After the doors shut, a smile lit up Probert's face as he made a wry comment as only he could. He proclaimed sincerely, "I always love elevators." Then he paused, letting that statement settle and build curiosity. "The doors close, and then," he said gleefully, just as the doors opened at our destination, "they open again in a new world." We burst out laughing at this simple observation.

He may have just been being silly, or reminiscing about the *Enterprise* turbolifts, but I think he was onto something deeper. It's that childlike magic of the doors opening into a new world that is at the core of scene transitions. It's the way you, as the filmmaker, bring the audience to that new world that makes all the difference.

ON THE SET

There's no such thing as a Transition Artist brought in to save a production. There is no guy that specializes in spectacular transitions that everybody calls up in a crisis. (Though, hey, after this I may apply for the position). It's mostly going to be up to the director to put these transitions into the film and use them as storytelling tools. The writer can pave the way by suggesting them in the script, and the editor can use them to spark ideas for the director. Actors think about transitions, too, when they create backstory and off-screen events to help find character motivation. The director may even assign the storyboard artist the task of thinking up transitions. Yes, even sound technicians might think of ways audio can be used to bridge scenes. Everybody on the production can think of them. But what exactly are transitions?

What I will show you are practical ways to enhance the telling of your story through the style of transitions you choose. You'll quickly become familiar with the possibilities available to you as the opening doors reveal — a new world.

ANATOMY OF A SCENE TRANSITION

"Without change there is no perception."

— WALTER MURCH, editor

Scene A	Scene B

A scene transition involves many different elements — so many, in fact, that they fill this book. First, it is the boundary generated between two scenes (we will refer to them as Scenes A and B) and reaches deep into the areas on either side of that boundary. It includes the movements of the characters, the revelation of plot information, as well as all visual, aural, and musical elements that play into shifts in time and space.

Most importantly, a scene transition is *change*. It is the moment where everything is in turmoil, and it's where the audience connects with the story. It is a shift from one state to another.

For the purposes of this book, a "scene" is an event which takes place at a single location. This event is a fight between two lovers, a villain planning his next move, a hero discovering that his kitchen cabinet is out of sugar — whatever action you've decided to encapsulate into a moment in time at a specific location.

The First Law of Scene Transitions is:

Scenes are events; transitions are the internalization of those events.

In other words, it's at the transitions that we are able to emotionally and intellectually process events and feel them on a visceral level.

Shape of Drama

Scenes all have similar shapes of drama, starting with an ebb and then building to a peak. This peak is generated by an increase in dramatic tension, as well as an increase in plot information. The endings of most scenes have a memorable *echo line* designed to linger in the viewers' minds while they're waiting

for the scene change. This line is presumably the nugget of plot that you want them to remember later or, as they come away from a scene, to think, "Oh, that's what that scene was about."

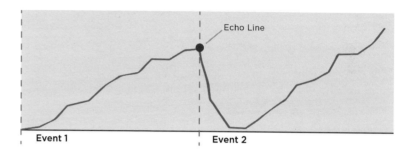

Each event is placed together with the other events, until we have groups of scenes called *sequences*. We assume the events are related in some way, either causally or comparatively. Otherwise, you don't really have a story.

Sequences also rise to a peak — a higher peak than the scene peaks — and they follow the same shape. Their echo lines are even more significant to the plot.

Keep in mind as you're going through your screenplay that not all scenes fit this easy cookie-cutter pattern. I've simplified it significantly to introduce the basics. If a scene in your screenplay doesn't have a clear event, it might be a transitional scene. Some entire scenes and sequences can actually serve as transitions between two bigger scenes. Chapter 8 will show you how to start puzzling different types of scenes together.

The Craft of Relief

The art of scene transitions is one of tension and release. Every scene is one wave in the series of waves which make up a film. By putting your scenes and sequences together, you create a series of dramatic waves. If you've ever built a sand castle on a beach when the tide was coming in, you've experienced the power of waves. The emotional contours of films are very similar. Emotional peaks tend to move things and shake them up, and ebbs tend to smooth them flat like the pure sand at the shoreline at the beach.

Feature films tend to be unique in the modern performance art world, in that they have no obvious breaks. TV and radio have commercials, the stage has curtain pulls, books have chapters, but feature films have no pauses to give the audience a rest. Thus the feature film storyteller must perform an act of trickery — to fool the audience into thinking there is no break while actually giving them a break. This is done by skilfully building periods of tension and release into your scene transitions.

Waves of tension and release in your story will tend to manifest themselves on screen through character reactions and scenery, respectively.

As you'll learn in Chapter 4, showing your hero in motion through geography is a common way to connect the audience with the hero's emotions. When a big plot event has just occurred, the hero reacts with tension, and if the audience is allowed to share in that reaction they will be pulled in. As a filmmaker, when you show the character on a journey (on a train, on horseback, in a car) it should have some sort of emotional meaning; otherwise it shouldn't be on the screen.

As you'll learn in Chapter 5, emotional ebbs are periods of release, giving the audience some downtime to think. You can give your audience a break by using scenery (see Chapter 5) and music (see Chapter 6). This pause to reflect will allow your viewers to shift to a new mindset in preparation for the next big event, and allow their imaginations to be absorbed deeper into the fictional story world.

By the Numbers

How many scenes should your film have? How many locations? There are no specific answers to these questions. It will depend on your budget and genre. More talky films that spend a lot of time with dialogue and character development are going to have less scenes than an action film that zips around in neighborhood chases. The number might range anywhere from 40 to 200 scenes in an average feature film.

These numbers are then grouped into larger sequences which will most likely range around 10 to 30 sequences per film.

The number of locations on a film will be a lot less than the number of scenes, because you tend to return to key locations throughout a story. Average location numbers range from 1 to about 30 depending on the budget. Again, chase films are going to rack up more locations.

When it comes to looking at scene transitions, these numbers are useful because it means more or less work in deciding how the transitions will go. As a result, you may decide during the process of creating scene transitions that you can synthesize your film down to fewer scenes and locations. Probably a good thing!

For example, the script I'm working on now has 30 sequences divided into 126 total scenes, in 20 locations. Most of those scenes are crosscut between each other, so they're being counted more than once. Generally there are about 40 actual whole scenes in such a script.

If you spend time worrying about all 126 of your scene transitions, you won't have time for anything else. Hopefully with this book, you'll learn which transitions are important so you can focus on the big ones. The rest will just come naturally, while you're doing other things like script analysis. Later in this chapter we'll go through the six major transitions you will want to remember.

Functions and Audience

Primarily, scene transitions fulfill these four functions:

1. Make audience think
2. Make audience feel
3. Give audience relief or build tension
4. Connect audience with character

Notice that each one of these functions contains the word "audience." Like Alfred Hitchcock said, the feelings of the audience are of utmost importance. All of the decisions you make at the scene transitions should be based on how the audience is going to feel as a result.

You can film all the characters you want in all the scenes that you want, and have them verbally state your plot for the audience. But the audience isn't going to care about any of it unless you connect them emotionally with the lead character. Your scene transitions are where this connection happens.

Scene transitions are the primary way to form an emotional bond between character and viewer. The reason: reactions to events.

The viewers see the event on screen, and if you allow them to share in the character's reactions to the event, they will be with you until the last scene and beyond.

CHOICES AT THE TRANSITION

In order to achieve the four functions, there is an infinite combination of choices to be made at every transition.

The screenplay/film that you're working on probably already has many of the features that we'll explore. The important thing is to recognize them and figure out how to clarify them. That way you can use them to your advantage to connect further with your audience.

Not every scene transition is going to need something special. However, if you keep the art of transitions in mind while you're working, it soon becomes a natural part of your craft. You'll think about it when you're choosing locations, editing the script, rehearsing with the actors, and in some cases before you even have a story.

By definition, all scene transitions are shifts in time and location. The ways that you show those shifts depend on how obvious you want them to be, and how you want your story to flow emotionally.

Scene transitions include the following dramatic possibilities:

• Creating boundaries between your locations
• Creating a feeling of loss or closure after a scene
• Tying one event to the next
• Showing the hero's journey from one scene to the next
• Showing the villain's journey
• Giving the audience a break
• Showing scenery
• Shifting a mood
• Using music to bridge scenes
• Considering the duration of the next scene
• Cutting out entire scenes to provoke thought
• Adding optical styles to the cut between scenes
• Clarifying the passage of time

Deciding whether to use these possibilities will involve the needs of the story and how it's absorbed emotionally by your audience.

Withhold or Behold, Tease or Please

Every style of scene transition in this book could be used in your next film. But you have to decide whether a specific transition technique is really necessary for each moment under question. Some scene changes are more important than others. Every decision you make at a scene change is about a degree of emphasis.

A film is a lot like an iceberg. It has thousands of elements, but you have to decide which to bring to the surface and which to submerge for the sake of clarity. It is the job of the filmmaker to bring to the screen only those few elements that are needed to tell a succinct story, burying the rest. If you just put anything and everything on the screen your story will get lost at sea. Many of your scene transitions should remain underwater — subtle and quick. Save the more obvious transitions for the important moments in your story. These can be drawn out and dramatic.

The simplest transition would be a shock cut which leaves the audience guessing. It may suffice in most of your scene changes.

On the other hand, entire new scenes and sequences can be manufactured to bridge two major scenes. These bridge scenes typically show a hero in motion from one place to another, usually showing an emotional reaction of some kind. In Chapter 9 we'll look at one of the longest scene transitions in film history — totaling eight minutes — from the movie *Gladiator*. (If you know of a longer one, e-mail me at info@borgus.com.)

With every transition technique in this book I'll show you both extremes — what happens if you use it and what happens when you don't.

THE LIFE OF A SCENE TRANSITION

"A screenplay is a story told in scenes, each scene necessary to tell the story. At this stage you're just testing if each scene is necessary. When planning a screenplay, I try to write the story in prose first, without dialog, with each scene represented by either a sentence or a paragraph. Then I read and revise the condensed story, omitting what is unnecessary."

— GREG MARCKS, director, screenwriter

Let's take a journey through the lifespan of a film and see how scene transitions enter into the process at each stage. This book is tailored especially toward writers, directors, and editors. Each chapter begins with a note to each person. But, as mentioned earlier, other crewmembers can be brought in to provide input at every stage.

Writer's Transitions

Some transitions begin at the writing stage. When you're typing up the first draft, scenes naturally fall in place. You choose the locations of each scene — a choice that may be drastically changed in subsequent drafts, or by the circumstances of production and location availability.

In a recent *Screenwriting Magazine* interview, Stephen Gaghan proclaimed "transitions are everything in movies!" Gaghan is an Academy Award–winning screenwriter and director, known for his work on the features *Traffic* and *Syriana*.

When Gaghan begins writing, he likes to start with locations first. By arranging moments from each location next to one another, his stories emerge. While writing *Syriana*, he discovered that transitions are the most important element of any good film, before you even get to the story. He outlined this order of importance:

1. Transitions
2. Context
3. Character
4. Story

According to Gaghan, by starting with transitions and context, then putting the characters in, a story will emerge last. He is convinced that this approach "strips away formula." He comments, "It allows you to stay in the inspired brain, not the editorial brain with all the received wisdom of what movies have to be. It keeps you in that little magic garden where great stuff gets handed to you for nothing."

This approach might be a bit extreme for some, but it's a great perspective to begin our exploration of transitions. Whatever your approach is for writing, scene transitions will become an essential part of the process.

In this early-draft stage of your film's infancy, you can freely experiment with transitions and see what you can come up with. When a character needs to travel from one location to another, drama emerges. A few key scenes may surface that inspire amazing transitions. Keep an eye on those. You may decide that others don't work.

The more you learn the craft behind scene transitions, you'll begin to recognize what a good transition looks like, and its function in the storytelling process.

As you approach your final draft, before sending it off to a producer, go through it and look specifically at every transition and bridging scene in your screenplay. Here are some things to ask yourself about each transition:

1. Are the locations opposites? (indoor/outdoor, day/night)

2. When the hero reacts to big news, do we get to follow his reaction?

3. When the bad guy is arriving, do we get to see it?

4. Are there objects that join the end of one scene to the beginning of the next scene?

5. Does each scene connect with a cause/effect hook, or a question/answer?

You'll discover the answers in subsequent chapters.

Director's Transitions

By the time a transition gets to the directing stage, it is the director who decides whether it survives or is cut. As the director, you have the final call on how all the transitions operate, because they are in the realm of visual storytelling and the artistic means to get there. Hopefully, the writer has tidied up the transitions for you already. If not, now is the time to start looking at them.

On your very first read of the screenplay, you should be taking notes about which moments are the most emotional and about the kind of moods you're feeling with each scene. Those emotional feelings won't ever come back as strong as they will on your first read, so now is the time to make note of all of them. Mark each emotional plot shift and character change with a symbol you'll recognize. I always use the Greek delta triangle (Δ), the mathematical symbol for change.

Now, somewhere in the midst of you preparing your shot lists and actors' backstories, spend a day going through all of your transitions — every change from one scene to the next. Note them in your shot lists.

As the director, you should make a list of all the plot revelations throughout the entire film divided into an appropriate number of sequences. Between each sequence make a note of what the transition will look like, so when you're shooting you will know how they go together at a glance.

The important thing to remember is that you must decide at each transition how much emphasis the transition is going to need. Most transitions suffice as just simple shock cuts, but others — the more emotional ones — need to be drawn out into something more elaborate.

The moments where you made a note (Δ) of a big emotion on your first read-through are probably where your bigger transitions are going to follow.

Make sure you know where every character goes between every scene. Consider that during an emotional moment you may want to show this journey on screen. Conversely, there may be journeys in the script that have no emotional component at all. Consider whether they are even necessary to show.

You'll want to have a solid grasp as to the rhythms of your film — where all the tension is and where it's released. Tension and release will play a big role in your decisions whether to show establishing shots between scenes and how to use music.

Here's your director's checklist:

1. Look for emotional moments where you felt something.

2. Look for major plot revelations, something that wildly shifts your perspective on the story.

3. Figure out where the hero moves from one location to another and ask whether it's portraying an emotion.

4. Look for overall rhythms of tension and release. Your sequences will emerge as soon as you pin these down.

At the end of the day, the art of transitions is the only aspect of filmmaking that the director is expected to decide on his own. Everyone else on your team is going to be thinking about individual scenes, actors, props, and the script pages. You're the only one that keeps the overall film in perspective and controls how those scenes flow together into a larger whole.

Editor's Transitions

By the time the transitions get to the editor (you in this case), the elements have already been put on film — hopefully. It's your job as editor, then, to make sure they work properly. Many ideas for transitions that made it this far simply do not work in the edit.

Most likely it will be up to you when to use dissolves and shock cuts, and it's time for you to play around with various options. Your job will be the art of *ellipses* — cutting things out and making the omission seamless.

The editor should play around with possibilities and note where something doesn't feel right. Perhaps you feel there needs to be an establishing shot between scenes to provide some relief. If it hasn't been shot, you may need to convince the director to go out and shoot the establishing shot.

It's very possible that you may enter production where the director hasn't thought of transitions at all before the editing phase. Sometimes there's such a mad rush to get everything done that it's easy to overlook. The result is that you're handed 130 disconnected scene capsules completely unrelated to each other. This means you'll have to do a lot of the creative work on the transitions and suggest plenty of options in the editing room.

Keep in mind that by this stage the director is most likely too close to the material. It's been months or years since he first read the script and he's seen this stuff so many times that he forgets what is actually on the screen and what isn't. Even if it's right in front of him, he'll think something is there when it's not. Be his pal and help him through it. If there is a stale sequence that just isn't working, suggest some alternatives. Crosscutting two separate sequences together can sometimes provide tension that didn't exist before. A collage with music may provide an emotional depth that was missing, or provide a way to take shortcuts in abbreviating a series of events.

Your editor's checklist:

1. Is there enough emotion at the end of each scene?

2. Does the emotion from one scene merge well into the mood of the next?

3. Is there enough tension and release?

4. Do the scenes flow well rhythmically as a whole?

In finding the perfect transitions, it's a collaboration between the editor and the director.

Viewers' Transitions

Once the transition has been locked into the final film, the viewers most likely won't notice it. If it works properly, the viewers will be pulled into the hero's world and connect with him emotionally. They won't know why.

The viewers' feelings and thoughts are the most important consideration. You can't just place an actor on screen and expect the audience to care. The connection between actor and audience isn't automatic. Moments must be built in to allow the audience to follow a hero's reaction to plot events. If the reaction is believable and familiar, they'll follow.

SIX MAJOR TRANSITIONS

"If the boy and girl walk off into the sunset hand-in-hand in the last scene, it adds 10 million to the box office."

— GEORGE LUCAS, director

I want to save you some time, especially since you have other things to worry about.

While your feature film will have dozens of important transitions from one scene to the next, there are six major transitions that you should not ignore. It's a good idea to focus on these six first, before looking at the others. Who knows, you may run out of time before getting to the others.

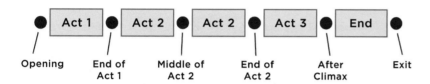

Find these moments in your screenplay/film and start thinking of ways you can draw the audience in.

Opening

The first transition in your film is the opening scene. It is the way you choose to bring the audience from reality into your fictional world of drama. You may choose to open *in medias res* or show a gradual buildup of story creeping into scenery. The most common opening transition shows a hero in motion, going somewhere. Showing bits and pieces of scenery edited rhythmically is also a common way to set the stage.

End of Act 1

This is an important moment where the plot has just kicked

in and your hero sets sail on a journey. A moment like this should most certainly be looked at in terms of bringing the transition forward to make it obvious. You'll want to create a way for the audience to internalize this moment and share it with the hero.

Middle of Act 2

It's not uncommon to hear screenwriters and filmmakers talk about the Act 2 reversal. This is a moment in the middle of your film where things shift in an entirely new direction for your hero. It's another important moment for the character and your transition should reflect the emotion.

End of Act 2

This is the point where everything is at its worst and things are getting desperate for our hero. When he begins to make steps toward his final showdown, the transition at this point is essential.

After Climax

There is a tender moment just after the climax when everything has been fixed and all the tension has been released. Immediately following this moment are the aftermath scenes for dangling plot threads to be tidied up. There is usually a transition between these two moments which shifts the mood. It might even be the climax itself which serves as this transition.

Exit

Often forgotten is the transition away from the fictional story world and back to reality. There are numerous creative ways that filmmakers handle the end credits. Sometimes it can be as simple as a cut to credits, popularized by George Lucas.

I'm not going to tell you that there's some magic formula for designing these six transitions, because there isn't. These transitions can be anything. It might be the arrival of the villain that you choose to emphasize at the end of Act 1. Or, it might be the hero getting onto a train and going somewhere. Your transition could be a long scenery shot, or a sudden jolt of black screen. It could be an entire transitional scene all in itself. As you read this book, you'll unlock your creative powers to make these six transitions spectacular.

TRANSITIONS BETWEEN SEQUENCES AND SCENES

After the major six, the next set of important transitions are those between sequences. Generally these are rhythmic breaks in tension. A sequence is a series of scenes which flow together through unifying tension and build to a climax. After each sequence you'll want to build in some sort of pause to reflect, either with scenery or a distracting subplot.

Everything left over after the Act and Sequence transitions are those transitions between scenes. As you'll see in Chapter 6, this also includes combining scenes by crosscutting several together, or putting them all on the screen simultaneously like in *Timecode*. The style of cutting between scenes can generate an overall attitude or mood.

As shown in the illustration below, a transition at an act junction is going to be a more significant emotion than the ones at the sequence junctions preceding it. The emotion at the sequence junction is going to be bigger than the scene junctions before it.

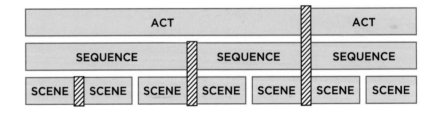

GRAB YOUR SCRIPT

Let's dive into your transitions. For the most part you'll learn which transitions in your story are the most important and which are unnecessary. You'll find that with a focused approach, you can make the important moments sing and de-emphasize the others to make things flow smoothly.

To help guide your choices, ask yourself this simple question: How can my transitions help forge a connection between my audience and my characters.

First, let's get an estimate of the number of transitions you should focus on in your script.

• Find your six major transitions.

• Now pinpoint all the other major emotional moments where your hero faces emotional change.

• Find all the big moments where your villain sets something in motion.

• How many transitions did you count? This number should be somewhere around 20 or 30. Focus on these transitions as you go through this book.

Next, by shaping your transitions in a certain way, you can strengthen your audience's bond with your story. As a result, your audience will feel your story in a more visceral way. The chapters ahead will demonstrate the tools you'll need.

CHAPTER TWO

CHOOSING LOCATIONS THAT COLLIDE

*"The more alert the audience is at those moments of transition,
the greater the opportunity we have to reveal things to them."*

— WALTER MURCH, editor

Locations interact. Locations communicate with each other. Locations create contrast and emphasis when placed next to each other. Locations create moods and emotions, they signal loss and change, they put pressure on characters, and they affect the viewer in profound ways.

To Writers: Most good stories are not location-specific. They could take place anywhere at any time. Be prepared for directors to come along and shuffle your locations. That's not to say that you shouldn't worry about them at all. You should. More times than not, a director will use the writer's location ideas. While the location choices are typically the purview of the director and the production staff (with budgetary concerns always on the front burner), as the writer you have power simply because you are the first person to summon up these ideas into everyone else's minds.

To Directors: It's usually one of the first big decisions a director has to make: location choices. As director you're the artist, holding a paintbrush over the canvas. The choices you make here can determine how an audience perceives your completed film. One thing you'll learn having gone through this book is that choosing a setting is more than aesthetics and symbolizing character desires. Location choices affect how the viewers feel as the scenes flow past them, and even how they remember the events that transpired.

To Editors: By the time the film gets to you, the locations have already been chosen and recorded onto film (or flash drive). So why should you care about location choices at this

point? It's your choice of when to use establishing shots — how long to hold them and when not to show them. (We'll get more into relief in Chapter 5.) Maybe you have an idea that could fix a flow problem like swapping two scenes, or adding a new establishing shot. Knowledge of how locations influence each other and the emotional flow through the film is what makes you a prized editor.

SCENEQUAKES

"In many ways, the grammar of film is up for grabs. Anyone can try a new way of juxtaposing shots to tell a story."

— MARTIN SCORSESE, director

When you place two scenes next to one another, a boundary is inherently formed.

If each scene is in a different location, drama is generated from the "friction" between these two locations. Think of Earth's tectonic plate boundaries when they generate earthquakes as they clash against each other. When the rocks are tough and jagged, a lot of force is released from the friction. This is the kind of energy that scene tectonics create. It's a collision which holds immense storytelling power.

Collision is what happens when two ideas are juxtaposed and the result is greater than the sum of the parts. When two dissimilar scenes are placed together sequentially, you are forced to compare and contrast them.

You want the audience to feel a change. By provoking and prodding the audience with a brief feeling of shock or disorientation, you can make the story stick in their emotions.

COLLISION WITH OPPOSITIONS

At some point in your life you may have played chess. Don't worry, I'm not going to ask you to remember the rules for each piece; but you probably do remember that one player has dark pieces and the other player has light ones. Because of this stark value contrast between the two players, it is always easy to determine at a glance where the opponents' pieces are and where they can move.

Now imagine that both players had white pieces and the entire chess board was white. What a disaster that would be! You'd spend all your time trying to figure out who owns the pieces and squares and very little time strategizing your next move. Clearly, for ease of playing the complicated game of 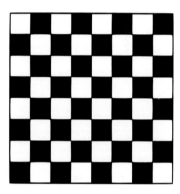 chess, contrast is essential. The same rule applies to the location choices in your film — something that storytellers have known for centuries. It's a phenomenon called *binary opposition*.

If it weren't for Ferdinand de Saussure, a Swiss linguist from the late 1800s, we wouldn't know about binary opposition. His parents were scientists and spent most of their time categorizing rocks and insects; thus his mind was trained to organize things at an early age. If he walked into your house, he would probably start organizing your DVD collection. Saussure developed much of the understanding of language that we still use today, specifically the ways the brain makes sense of symbols and codes.

It was Saussure who postulated that the mind makes sense of a concept by comparing it against what it is not. As Saussure is often quoted:

"Concepts are… defined… negatively by their relations with other terms of the system. Their most precise characteristic is in being what others are not."

In other words, when we see something new, we first make note of what it isn't, ruling out all possibilities before we decide what it is. This is another way of saying that opposites make it easier for us to figure things out. It's a form of shorthand.

As you'd expect, great writers throughout the centuries commonly categorized story elements into pairs of opposites for ease of interpretation. That goes for locations, too. Even Leo Tolstoy used contrasting locations in his epic novel *War and Peace.*

The underlying implication is that storytellers are best served using oppositions for the sake of clarity; one thing is defined against another. Just like on the chess board.

Applied to location choices of feature films, we would expect to find oppositions from one scene to the next, e.g., day to night, indoor to outdoor, city to country, close-up to wide, solitude to crowd, quiet to loud, etc. And we do. Look for it the next time you watch a good film.

The visual and audio properties of each scene surrounding the transition tend to use binary oppositions. Shifting from one to the other provokes the viewer into thought.

So when you sit down to plan your locations, start thinking about oppositions. They can open up a world of possibilities that you probably wouldn't think about normally. Oppositions do three things, as I'll show you next.

Demarcate the Scene Boundary

Just like on the chess board, oppositions between two locations create dramatic lines of demarcation around scenes.

When switching from one scene to the next in Crash, *director Paul Haggis used binary oppositions.*

We know when a scene has changed because the new scene is drastically different. The juxtaposition of two scenes inherently prompts the viewer to compare the two. The viewer's mind is engaged. It tells us that there are two separate events to be considered in relation to one another.

For an example of this, Paul Haggis utilizes oppositions almost exclusively in the scene transitions of *Crash* (2004), a film about the racial rifts in a contemporary American city. Haggis switches between outdoor and indoor scenes at nearly every transition, and on exceptions where he goes from indoor to another indoor scene, the lighting is significantly different, e.g., dark to light. He also juxtaposes scenes along the lines of upper class vs. lower class, authority vs. criminal, minority vs. white, etc.

Provoke Meaning

> *"Creativity grows from the broken places."*
>
> — JULIE BURSTEIN, radio host

These contrasts of aesthetic from Scene A to Scene B mutually help to define each locale against its opposite, and thus generate a meaning not inherent in the two when considered separately. We internalize the race boundaries, for instance, in *Crash* due to their emphasis, just like we internalize the class boundaries in *Titanic* (1997) when director James Cameron juxtaposes scenes from the upper and lower decks.

It doesn't even have to be the locations themselves, but the aesthetic choices within them that can be contrasted. Cutting from a loud scene to a soft scene has dramatic power and vice versa.

The Fountain (2006), directed by Darren Aronofsky, follows a hero who exists in three different time periods, thousands

FUTURE

PRESENT

PAST

of years apart. The boundaries between these time periods are are created primarily by contrasting wardrobe and hair styles of Tom (Hugh Jackman.)

As seen in the photos to the left, Tom's appearance is different in each time period. For example, his head is bald in the future, he has average hair in the present, and he has long hair with beard in the ancient past. Viewers watching this film automatically know which time period is being shown simply by looking at Tom.

Furthermore, viewers can draw other comparisons due to the contrasts created in Tom's demeanor and personalities. The audience can internalize Tom's poor health in *The Fountain's* future because it is juxtaposed with his healthy present-day self, and can more readily notice Tom's scientific intellect in the present because it is being juxtaposed by his primitive ignorance in the past timeline.

Aronofsky utilizes this demarcation of character in order to blur the boundaries between time periods. In one instance Aronofsky cuts from a close-up of Tom in the future time period to a reaction shot of Isabel (Rachel Weisz) in the present. He then continues to mix and match reaction shots from each time period to create a continuously flowing conversation, conveying a sense that this is all happening in Tom's mind.

Stark opposites in hairstyles and clothing demarcate time period and character traits in Darren Aronofsky's *The Fountain*.

Punctuate the Previous Event

You can use a scene boundary's aesthetic jolt to serve as punctuation to emphasize an important moment or to generate a comic laugh. The sudden juxtaposition from Scene A to B punctuates the last moments of Scene A.

In *Titanic*, early scene junctions utilize this bombardment of punctuation through juxtaposition. For example, old Rose (Gloria Stuart), a Titanic survivor, proclaims "the woman in the picture is me" at the end of Scene A, and immediately Cameron cuts to Scene B with a swell of music as a helicopter flies into frame over an endless blue ocean. The punctuation effect causes her line to echo in the viewer's mind. Similarly, Cameron utilizes the loud, shocking sound of the ship's foghorn to introduce another Scene B, simultaneously punctuating a final line from Scene A.

SUDDEN ABSENCE

You can give a scene emphasis through its sudden absence. This is what I call the *bubble theory*. When one scene disappears we are prompted to consider what it once was, and we define the new presence of Scene B first by the mere fact that it is not Scene A.

When the scene is completely gone we can see its entire form, just like when a bubble is cut off from its source and becomes a sphere. It's now a whole scene. We see the scene's shape and form completely because it's no longer on screen.

There is a moment when the new scene comes in that we are still thinking about the previous scene. It is only when the new scene grabs our attention that we shift our focus.

This bubble theory is often used as punctuation when a line from the end of Scene A echoes in the viewer's mind simply because the source of the line (the actor) is no longer present on the screen. This is the echo line that is planted into the viewer's mind to consider during the scene transition. It has the effect of staying present in the mind because it was the last thing we heard before the scene disappeared.

Cut to Black

Anyone who saw the last episode of *The Sopranos* can tell you the most extreme form of transition anyone can make is to cut to black and hold it.

When you use a black screen between two scenes, it forces the most extreme form of this phenomenon. It's a jolt. That's why you see it so often in movie trailers.

It also clearly separates ideas. Anything that happens after the black screen is considered completely disconnected from the previous. It renders any binary opposition you've created useless, because the black screen is a location in itself. It is a place of nothingness.

Cutting to black forces the viewer to contemplate the meaning of *what was*. If the scene had continued, the viewer would still be contemplating *what is*, perhaps anticipating more action.

Cutting to black stops time. It is the absence of content and the absence of story. It places a harsh boundary at the end of the scene, provoking the viewers to think about what just happened. It takes the viewers out of the story.

White Screen

On the opposite end of the spectrum is the white screen. Where black is considered to be an absence of story and time, cutting (or most likely fading) to white is an overwhelming intensity of story. White represents an overload of story, e.g.,

a spiritual transcendence in *The Fountain*. Rather than time stopping, a white screen is fully present in the moment. It is generally not considered to be a boundary from one scene to the next, but more like a bridge. The viewer doesn't tend to feel a jolt, rather hangs on to see what's coming.

ADD MORE DRAMA TO BOUNDARIES

There are ways that the boundaries you've generated between two scenes can be enhanced even further. By utilizing actual fences, walls, and doorways in your setting you can impose the scene boundaries on your heroes. When the characters want to go to the next scene, they must overcome the barrier. They must work dramatically to cross from one scene to another.

The Coen Brothers' Miller's Crossing *includes doorways in nearly every scene.*

Doorways

The Coen Brothers brought a harsh physicality to the scene boundaries in *Miller's Crossing* (1990), creating a sense of real boundaries existing within the story space, imposing closed doors at nearly every movement from Scenes A to B.

Door knocking in *Miller's Crossing* is utilized as a means of permission to enter a space at the beginning of scenes, and door slamming as a means of punishment.

If your characters frequently slam doors when they leave and arrive, it creates a harsh boundary aesthetic. This boundary can be used as an intimidation device between characters, and the corresponding sound serves as metaphorical gunshot to unsettle the viewer.

The characters can use the scene boundaries to block *each other* as well. In *Miller's Crossing*, Bernie (John Turturro) knocks on the door to Verna's (Marcia Gay Harden) apartment at the beginning of a scene, she opens it and then slams it in his face. He knocks again, and this time she lets him in. Later, Tom (Gabriel Byrne) knocks on Verna's door, and they both struggle with the wooden door before he pushes his way into the scene.

Breaking through doors to begin a scene is another common device in *Miller's Crossing*, as Tom bursts through double doors to speak to Verna, announcing, "Close your eyes ladies! I'm comin' in!"

Watch *Miller's Crossing* and see how many uses of doorways you can find.

In chapter 4 we'll take a closer look at what happens when characters cross the boundaries. When the distance between two locations is vast, they must travel across geography to reach the next scene. This can be used to emotional advantage in your script.

Chopping Up the Screen

Boundaries like the ones in Mike Figgis' *Timecode* (2000) and Joel Schumacher's *Phone Booth* (2002) actually divide the scenes on the frame simultaneously, blurring the traditional boundaries of scene transitions. In *Timecode*, the screen is divided into four equal parts displaying four separate locations in apparent real time, while the audio is mixed to manipulate viewer attention.

Mike Figgis' *Timecode* puts the scene boundaries on the screen.

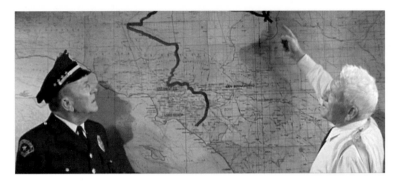

Scenes are inserted as on-screen squares in Phone Booth, *directed by Joel Schumacher.* © 2002 Twentieth Century-Fox. All rights reserved.

Some films put a map of the story world on the screen to help the audience visualize the plot movement in their minds, like this example from It's a Mad, Mad, Mad, Mad World, *directed by Stanley Kramer.* © 1963 United Artists Films. All rights reserved.

Phone Booth utilizes various sized inserts of shots within the screen composition to show both sides of a phone call simultaneously, much like a conversation on a cable news broadcast. These scene boundaries tend to call more attention to their presence.

MENTAL MAPS

If a father and his son get lost in a corn maze (which sometimes happens in the Midwest), they will eventually find the single best solution: The boy stands on his father's shoulders and from this elevated vantage point gives Dad directions to the nearest exit. Your movie may be just as confusing as the corn maze, so it's nice to help the viewer along. Give them a map.

Some movies, like *It's a Mad, Mad, Mad, Mad World* (1963) and *EuroTrip* (2004), actually show the map on screen. Most movies are sneaky though, and put each story event at a recognizable and unique location to help the viewers create a map in their minds. Each location has its own event. No two events happen in the same location unless there's a connection to be made between them. Going back to a location for a second event had better be connected somehow to the first event, otherwise the viewer will be trying to find a connection that isn't there.

Mentally mapping the story through a unique array of locations is a way to easily compartmentalize events and connect the events together to make logical sense.

In *The Wizard of Oz* (1939) for instance, we all have a general idea of where Munchkin Land is in relation to the Emerald City, with the forest in between. We deduce that the Wicked Witch of the West's castle must then be somewhere to the west of everything else. The fact that Glinda (played by Billie Burke) is the Good Witch from the North and the dead witch is from the east makes it easy. We spend little effort trying to piece together this geography in our minds.

The clear demarcation of *The Wizard of Oz*'s geography helps us make sense of it all. Furthermore, we know that the forest is scary and the poppy field will put a person to sleep. Each of these locations contains story features that push the characters and help us internalize the events. We know if Dorothy (played by Judy Garland), for some reason, decided to go back to Munchkin Land, more or less she would be safe and protected, because the filmmaker has created that sense for us. And, of course, we get a sense that Kansas is ordinary — no frills — because it's filmed in black and white.

SINGLE-LOCATION FILMS

Let's say your film takes place entirely in one location. How do you create boundaries between your scenes?

Alfred Hitchcock's *Rope* (1948) and *Lifeboat* (1944) both take place entirely in one location. Even though there are no boundaries between locations, the action within those films does include a level of demarcation.

Rope includes cuts on moments of important emphasis as well as ellipses generated by zooming into a character's back, or onto an object. The boundaries within *Rope* are therefore subtle shifts in perspective within the same space. Characters in *Rope* move to a new room within the apartment when something new happens.

Lifeboat includes differences between night and day, and changes in weather — both serving the purpose of demarcating a dramatic boundary.

Gus Van Sant's *Gerry* (2002) takes place in a desert from start to finish. He uses stark differences in landscape, time of day, camera movement, editing speed, and mood. These differences create scene boundaries, and the landscape changes demarcate growing and changing moods.

Since there is very little plot in *Gerry*, the changing landscape reveals a loosely held narrative of connecting emotional states. *Gerry* was filmed in three separate deserts — starting in Argentina, then Utah, and California — all representing the same desert. This gives you a rich topography and allows a transformation of moods to take place over time.

- serene

- dynamic and alive

- puzzled and lost

- turning angry, sad, and turbulent

- finally it spills out onto a flat emotionless wasteland

These emotional states are achieved primarily through location choices and camera movements edited in such a way as to cue the viewer to internalize them.

GRAB YOUR SCRIPT

Now take a look through your script and notice how your locations fit together. Ask yourself these questions:

- Is each of my locations unique enough to be remembered alongside all the other locations?

- Do all the combined locations in my script create a vivid mental map for the audience?

- Have I used enough contrast from one location to the next in order to provoke the audience to find meaning, or punctuate a previous event?

- Are there any moments in my script that would benefit from sudden absence (a quick cut from a scene to make the audience feel loss and closure).

- Can I create more drama by imposing doorways, windows, or other boundaries on my characters?

- Do my location choices throughout my story reflect the changing moods of my hero?

CHAPTER THREE

TYING YOUR EVENTS TOGETHER

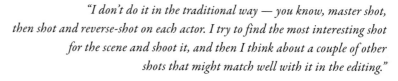

"I don't do it in the traditional way — you know, master shot, then shot and reverse-shot on each actor. I try to find the most interesting shot for the scene and shoot it, and then I think about a couple of other shots that might match well with it in the editing."

— TIM BURTON, director

You can't just throw together random events and hope they make sense. Those scenes which you carefully placed next to each other should connect in some way. Your series of events should be tied together like the stitches holding together a patchwork quilt, or life rafts roped together at sea.

To Writers: Tying your events together is what storytelling is all about. Coming up with clever ways to connect your scenes is where the fun is.

To Directors: Ultimately it's your choice what shots you put next to each other when leaving one scene and going into the next. This chapter will show you ways to think about using techniques to link scenes together. You may decide that the connectors written into the script work well, or maybe aren't necessary. The editor will probably come up with some good ideas, too, or she will tell you that your scene connectors are too obvious or corny to use. Use them sparingly, only for the best moments.

To Editors: Out of everything else in this book, this is probably on the top of the list for you to consider. You should ask: "How do I create a smooth flow from one scene to the next?" Here we explore this concept of linking scenes together, visually, aurally, and narratively. Hopefully, this will provide you with a basic craft which you can pull from when you're problem-solving under pressure in the editing room.

THE TRAIN

Film events are a lot like a train. Each event is being pulled one after another, connected to each other in a series. If one becomes disconnected, everything after it will roll to a stop.

When I was a kid I remember riding an Amtrak train from Missouri to California with my grandma. The two-day trip was quite exhausting for the attention span of a young child, which left my imagination flowing. My favorite train activity was walking from car to car through the double doors. Each door was controlled by a button, and the door made a whoosh sound when I pressed the button to open it. I imagined I was on a space station and had to open an airlock to pass into each capsule.

Just like train cars are latched together by couplers, film events are connected by a process called *linkage*. It has been called other things as well. Whatever you want to call it — linkage, continuity editing, unity, cohesion, the hook — each scene is connected in some way to the one after it.

Linkage is a way of letting the viewer pass through the airlock and venture into the next imaginary world, without falling off the train.

It was a Russian director, Vsevolod Pudovkin, who came up with the idea of linkage in the early days of film. You could venture to guess that his background in chemistry gave him a unique mindset in looking at film editing. Just like atomic elements stick together in chemical bonds, Pudovkin saw that film shots have similar ways of linking together. His filmmaking friends didn't agree with his ideas at first, because they were so excited about creating collisions between their scenes with their theory of montage. A good film needs a combination of both.

LINKING THROUGH SIMILARITY

Luckily, the human mind likes to find patterns and associations. If there are any similarities to be found between two adjacent scenes, the brain will notice. In the BBC documentary *Space Age: NASA's Story*, the editor cleverly cuts from people being interviewed to past footage of their younger selves in action. I could easily see that the 80-year-old retired NASA scientist was the same person that was shown sitting in the 1970s Apollo control room. And nobody had to tell me it was the same person. I just knew. Why? Because my brain saw the

similar facial features immediately, even though they were 40 years apart.

Linking Objects

The most famous scene transition of all time, hands down, is the flying bone in Kubrick's *2001: A Space Odyssey* (1968) which turns into a space station. Kubrick cuts from the bone in Scene A to a flying space station in Scene B. Both look remarkably similar

A bone turns into a space station in Stanley Kubrick's 2001: A Space Odyssey.

in shape and motion. This visual connection bridges thousands of years by linking similarly shaped objects — instantly dramatizing the technological progress mankind had made over that time.

Let's say you have two adjacent scenes that you want to connect. Is there a prop in the first scene that could be shown in the second scene? *Titanic* is a goldmine for finding these kinds of linking techniques. Early in the film, the older Rose brings her goldfish with her on the helicopter, then Cameron cuts to the next scene inside the ship — a close-up of the fish bowl now sitting on a dresser. The presence of the fish bowl at the end of Scene A and the beginning of Scene B, especially with it being in a different location, serves as a visual hook. It also cleverly connects with the theme of being underwater.

And you can't miss Cameron's links between present and past, bridging a span of 80 years with simple object linkage. In this case the object is an entire ship — first shown on the ocean,

Using an object can connect the end of one scene with the beginning of the next, as seen with the fish bowl in James Cameron's Titanic.

Linking two time periods by showing the ravages of time. Titanic.

and then shown on the ocean floor. Link these together with a perfectly matching dissolve and you have the famous transition. Cameron dissolves smoothly from the freshly painted bow in 1912 to an exactly matching, rotting ship in the present day.

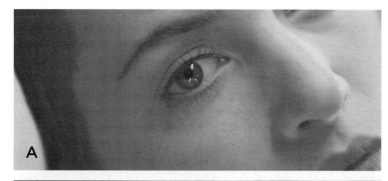

James Cameron links characters by blending facial features in Titanic.

Linking Characters

Cameron also links two actresses playing the same character

by using a dissolve between their eyes. Cameron brings us back to the present day through a close-up of young Rose's eye (A) as it transforms to her aged one (B) from Kate Winslet to Gloria Stuart.

Linking Locations

Linking locations is a bit trickier. If you put two similar locations next to each other, the viewer's mind will just assume that it's the same location in the same time.

Changing the soundscape is one way of linking similar locations. Much of the film *Offing David* (2008), which I directed and edited, takes place at a party with ambient music playing in the background. Each time we cut to a new location within the party house, the loudness of music jumps as well to help demarcate. Often times we would set a scene close to the music source, and the adjacent scene far away — the effect cutting on the same song from loud to quiet. When we jumped forward in time we made sure to cut to a new style of song to indicate time had passed. This way the audience feels the change, even if subconsciously.

If there's no clear demarcation between your locations, the audience will get confused (or bored), but maybe that's the effect you want — to convey a certain mood.

Linking Shots

There are many books, including Steven D. Katz' *Film Directing Shot by Shot*, that skillfully describe ways to join two shots through composition. This is a common technique in which both shots surrounding a transition have similar screen attributes. Smooth edits can also be made by matching motion from one shot to the next.

THE WRIGHT WIPE

Some ways of linking are just pure aesthetic tricks. Director Edgar Wright is known for using clever sleight-of-hand tricks to smoothly transition between scenes. In *Hot Fuzz* (2007) he uses a wipe hidden with the crossing of a person in front of the camera. The person is generally out of focus and in shadow, crossing the frame, providing just enough distraction to quickly wipe to the next scene. With an added sound (it might be a hiss or a gasp), the edit becomes as smooth as silk.

THE HOOK

Up until this point we've pretty much ignored the obvious — the story! The easiest way to link two scenes together is through story. Most people call this a hook.

Cause/Effect

The *hook* is an audiovisual device linking scenes through chains of cause and effect, in which a device at the end of Scene A (cause) is connected to a device at the beginning of Scene B (effect).

These hooks can be variations of audio or visual material, connecting both sides of the scene junction in a causal way, just like one train car is hooked to the back of another. Perhaps someone lights a match and the next scene begins with a raging fire. One scene ends with a gun shot and the next scene opens at a funeral. The viewer can easily establish their causal relationship through inductive reasoning.

Question/Answer

Commonly, the hook raises a question through a lingering line of dialogue and provides an answer either visually or through a connecting line of dialogue. Or action is promised and then the follow-through is shown in progress. This is one way that the echo line (see Chapters 1 and 2) can be used as a hook.

In *Titanic*, Jack (played by Leonardo DiCaprio) asks Rose (Kate Winslet), "so you want to go to a real party?" The question is answered as Cameron immediately cuts to the lower deck, alive with Irish music and dancing in which Rose is taking part. The answer to Jack's question is clear — she went to the party.

It may also be your tactic to raise a question at the end of a scene and intentionally avoid answering it in the next scene. This keeps the audience guessing and wondering what has been omitted (more about this in Chapter 8).

LINKING MULTIPLE PLOTS

Because of the recent merging styles of feature films and serial television, it is becoming quite common for films to include an amalgam of many plots. As a result, linkage becomes even more important in making sense of what all the random characters are doing.

This goes beyond the traditional movie hero formula. Two plot lines (essentially two films) that are seemingly unrelated can be put together to serve a comparative function. Sometimes there can be three, four, or, if you're really wild, five separate plots all being webbed together.

In fact, multiple plot lines, known as *network narratives*, draw from the concept of finding a metaphorical or even physical link between unrelated plots.

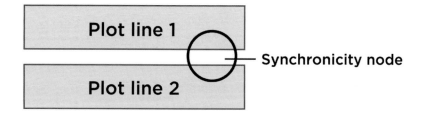

To link these multiple plot lines you must use what I call a *synchronicity node*: an object, location, or moment which links two or more separate plot lines by random coincidence.

Object

The rifle in Alejandro González Iñárritu's *Babel* (2006), the small statue in Haggis' *Crash* (2004), the bowling ball in Greg Marcks' *11:14* (2003), are all examples of transitional objects as synchronicity nodes which connect each film's multiple plot lines.

Location

A single location through which more than one plot line passes, such as the school corridor in Gus Van Sant's *Elephant* (2003) or the highway bridge in *11:14*, can also be a synchronicity node. These nodes act as a memory prompt to help the viewer piece together the linkage of the complex web of characters, and in the case of *Elephant* and *11:14* cue the viewer that time is being repeated from an alternate point of view.

Characters

Chance meetings by characters from two different plot lines are another common synchronicity node, such as LAPD cop John Ryan (Matt Dillon) saving Elizabeth's (Karina Arroyave) life in *Crash*, or the teenagers (Colin Hanks, Stark Sands, and Ben Foster) crashing their van into Cheri (Rachael Leigh Cook) in *11:14*. These chance encounters set up causal events which alter the course of the plot, compounding the meaning of each separate plot.

GRAB YOUR SCRIPT

Here are some questions to ask yourself about the script or film you are working on:

- Is each of my scenes connected in some way to the one after it?

- Are there scenes that can be linked by similar objects, locations, or by the same character?

- What kinds of creative matching shots can I use to link my scenes?

- Does my story do enough to link my scenes through cause/effect or question/answer hooks?

- If my script has multiple plots, where are my synchronicity nodes?

CHAPTER FOUR

EMOTIONAL PEAK: HERO IN MOTION

"They're moving pictures, let's make 'em move!"

— HOWARD HAWKS, director

We've all seen those old soap operas. The commercial is coming, something big has just happened, the actress is in shock, and the music swells up. It leaves us in suspense as the scene fades into the commercial break.

It all seems so clichéd and obvious that it's easy to dismiss. But there's something important happening there. Those little moments at the end of the scene are a goldmine for connecting with the viewer. In a feature film, you don't cut away to commercials. You get to show what the character does in reaction to big events. You follow them out to the car, around the block, or even to a different planet.

When we think of travel in real life, we tend to think of boredom. Waiting in traffic during rush hour, sitting through a long flight — these are all moments we'd rather forget. But for some reason, these moments of travel can be intently captivating in a movie narrative if they are expressing a character's emotion.

Director Zach Braff puts his character in motion in Garden State.

To Writers: This is probably the most important technique for you to consider. When we follow one of your characters in motion through geography, it has to be for an emotional reason. Pinpoint all the times in your script that a character is riding in a car, bus, train, etc., and figure out the emotion with which you want to connect the viewer. If there is none, take the scene out. Likewise, if there's a big emotional moment for your hero and it's not followed by a "road trip," maybe you should add one. This chapter should help you sort it out.

To Directors: For the director, this technique is among the most important to master, by far. You have to determine the best way to connect your hero with the audience. By showing your hero's reaction to plot events and following him in motion, you allow the viewer to connect. Just like I told the writers, find all the moments in your screenplay in which a character is in motion and ask what he's feeling. If the journey produces no emotion, should it really be on screen?

To Editors: There's probably not much you can do about this by the time the film gets to the editing room. But it might help you fix a problem in the edit. Let's say there's just not enough emotion during a scene transition. You may be able to puzzle some shots together that give more screen time to the hero's reaction to events — an extended close-up, stock footage of a car trip, steal a car trip from another scene, etc. This chapter will help you find ideas.

ON THE MOVE

In movies, characters move when they're reacting to big news. But as a storyteller you have to choose when to show it, and when not to. With more than 130 scene transitions in your new movie, it would get quite repetitive to show your hero getting into his car 130 times. You may not want to show it at all.

Zach Braff's *Garden State* is noteworthy for not showing the journey of Andrew (played by Zach Braff) from one place to another. A scene cuts and suddenly he's in a new place. Braff was clever in his role as director, because he was able to use this sort of abbreviation to portray the character's sense of mental disengagement. And because it is expressed by a lack of journeys between locations, the viewer feels it too.

But in *Garden State* there are those rare times Braff actually does show the character's journey between locations on a sidecar motorcycle. In these moments, the viewers feel the same sense of freedom as that felt by the character: They connect with the hero's emotion.

The Transport Scene

In the previous chapters you learned about the dynamic created by placing two scenes (two events at two locations) next to one another in sequence. The resulting boundary generated between the locations is ripe for the characters to cross dramatically.

Often you'll create an entire scene featuring the hero's emotional trip from one location to another. These are called *transport* scenes. They fit between two normal scenes and show a character (usually the hero or villain) moving through geography. The transport scene counts as one big scene transition. Read more on the different types of transitional scenes in Chapter 7.

LOOKING AT THE SCRIPT

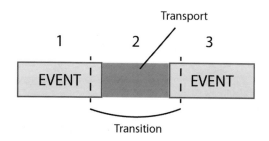

"The script is not everything. It's the interpretation that's everything — the visual interpretation of what you have on paper."

— MARTIN SCORSESE, director

So now you have your new script in hand and are ready to dive in. Probably the first thing you should look for are those moments of profound plot revelation. They most likely will occur at the end of a scene, or the end of a sequence. Make note of them, because now is the time to start thinking about how you'll handle the transition from that moment into the scene after it.

Throughout this book, the First Law of Scene Transitions is: *Scenes are events; transitions are the internalization of those events.*

If you're the director, make sure you know where all the journeys are in your movie — in and out of the script — because you'll be making a decision at every stage of the filmmaking process as to which journeys should be on screen. A journey, for these purposes, depicts a character moving from one location into another by physically traveling through geography. Presumably there is an inner journey happening as well. As such, some of these journeys might be goldmines of cinematic opportunity waiting to be discovered.

Go through your entire script and make note of where your hero moves from location to location. For instance:

Scene A features your hero in a park in the morning

Scene B has her shopping that afternoon

Where was she between those scenes? How did she get from the park to the shops? It's most likely not in the script, but your creative answers to those questions may spark an idea you can use.

Actors already know about this. They prepare for scenes by thinking about the off-screen events which happen before and after the scene in order to help them get "in the moment." As their director you'll probably be working with them to create this material as well. Now you have a new use for it. If you need to express a character emotion, these offscreen journeys are available to you to help make the character come to life.

Having said that, some of those geographic journeys might actually be in your script, but they may be easy to overlook. In a film I directed, *Offing David*, one of the longest and most suspenseful sequences arose from only one sentence in the script. We turned one line, "Richard follows them on the highway to the mountains," into a five-minute chase sequence.

As the director, not only will you be deciding what to show between the scenes, you'll be deciding how extravagant those journeys will be. It could be as simple as your character walking out the door, or as complex as a ten-minute on-screen journey to another continent.

When Maximus (played by Russell Crowe) escapes execution in Ridley Scott's *Gladiator* (2000), it takes him nearly ten minutes of screen time to arrive at the African province of Zucchabar on a stretcher. In between he walked, rode on horseback, camped through the night, went home, found his family murdered, fell asleep, got captured, and was hauled in a wagon across the desert. Some journey! Scott could have just cut to the desert immediately. Instead we get to experience the psychosis of Maximus' inner mind, and we are set up to savor his return to Rome later in the movie. For a closer examination of this sequence, see Chapter 9.

ANATOMY OF CHARACTER AT THE SCENE CHANGE

You must connect the audience to your film's story. The characters exist solely for this purpose. True storytelling is not about showing a slice-of-life, capturing realism, or showing events that are believable; these elements are all part of a style that you may be utilizing to evoke a mood. But if you miss the bigger point — that storytelling is about connecting the viewer with the plot — you fail. Storytelling is about the viewer falling momentarily in love with the person on the screen, relating with him or her on a visceral level, and thus "getting" the plot.

French director Jean-Luc Godard described it as the moment when a character's essence is superimposed on the plot. At the end of a scene there is a special moment when the two are fused, becoming one in the same. The character is relaying the plot to us, and the plot is relaying the character to us. It is a unified marriage in which the viewer is carried aloft, fully engaged.

More times than not, this connection between viewer and hero happens in those ripe and contemplative moments between scenes — where emotions are changing and drama is vibrant.

Let's walk through the typical scene transition in which a hero goes on a journey, both emotionally and geographically.

Something Big Just Happened

At the end of every scene, something big happens and we anticipate the effect it will have on the characters. It might be in the form of an echo line in dialogue that sparks a reaction or just some new discovery. It could be a piece of news that changes everything.

A film's plot is released in waves, just like waves of the ocean crashing onto a beach. The most intense release of plot is toward the end of every scene where the wave peaks and crashes onto the shore. Then the wave retreats and things get calm again. The next scene begins.

It's not enough that this "something big" has just happened, it also comes with an emotional charge. It tugs at our empathy. Film is, at its core, an emotional release of plot information. The characters give us that sense of emotion. The only reason the characters exist is to dramatically express that information so the viewer can internalize it.

I call this process the *engagement*.

Engagement is a plot revelation with the viewer's emotion added. It is a flow line that peaks at the end of the scene. Engagement can be defined as:

The varied flow of emotionally charged mental intensity by the viewer as they process fresh plot information. It is evoked from the specific events and actions in the movie as shaped by the storyteller.

This can be simplified into an easy formula:

Engagement = Plot Intensity + Emotional Charge

As a result, the plot peak and the emotional charge combine, causing us to engage emotionally with the events. The key here is that the character on screen must react.

The Character Reacts

The character is in shock, in the midst of making a profound decision, or taking an action prompted by what has just happened.

When the character reacts to plot information, he tends to move. As the wave of plot intensity increases and the engagement rises, the character jumps on his surf board and rides the wave to the shore (the shore is the beginning of the next scene).

Cinematically, it's common to show characters walking at this moment, or to put them in vehicles. You can put them in cars, trains, bicycles, motorcycles, buses, airplanes, spaceships... or on horseback. These means of transport allow characters to act with

Plot Intensity + Emotion

or against the emotional forces — either to escape or to pursue.

In *Garden State*, the hero, Andrew, jumps onto his motorcycle and hits the streets. His father has just insulted him, and the emotional sting causes him to walk out of the room and uncover his old motorcycle in the garage. He gets on and rides like mad down the dark suburban streets of his hometown. We feel his sense of freedom, escaping his father's oppression.

The Viewer Is Carried Aloft

When the "something big" happens and the hero gets on his surfboard to ride the plot wave, the engagement rises and the viewer is fully involved. The viewer is the most important consideration at every scene transition. You have to anticipate what they are thinking and feeling and how their mind is engaging the material.

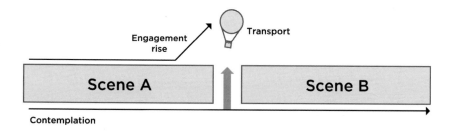

At this moment the viewer is carried aloft, swept away into the story, fully connected with the events and the character. The viewer rides the story like a hot-air balloon, being carried aloft by the emotions.

There are two mental states that the viewer has throughout a film — engagement and contemplation. If the director has done his job, these two states mirror the waves of plot intensity mentioned above. The viewer will be the most involved at the engagement *rise* of every scene (at the peak of the wave), and the most contemplative at the beginning of the next scene (when the water recedes from the beach).

That second, more reflective emotional state is what I call the contemplation. It is the opposite of engagement because it is defined by its lack of plot intensity. In fact, usually there is no fresh plot at all at the beginning of Scene B.

The contemplation is the more passive, objective processing of the events in the absence of fresh plot information, as suggested by moods and story context.

The engagement rise is the moment of emotion at the end of Scene A where the plot thickens, the character reacts, and the viewer's mind is fully aware of the plot. Engagement then dissipates and falls back into contemplation, such that the beginning of Scene B allows the viewer to relax and ponder the overall story and context without focusing on individual plot details. You'll learn more about the contemplation in the next chapter.

These two emotional states should be present on some level during every scene transition. Both can exist at the same time. This is where the true art of scene transitions arises. It's your job as writer, director, or editor to manipulate it in just the right combination in order to tell your story.

Here's an exercise to help you figure this out. Let's say a specific plot point at the end of your scene is:

Aunt Bell discovers she has run out of tea bags and must get more.

That's a normal plot point you'd expect. When looking at it on an emotional level, how will you be able to tell if you need to show Aunt Bell going on an emotional journey, or to just cut to the next scene where she's already at the grocery store? The key is to decide what you want the audience to feel when she discovers that she has run out of tea. To involve the viewer emotionally, the specific rise in engagement at the end of the scene would include further information:

Aunt Bell discovers she is out of tea bags and the audience connects with her emotional reaction through laughter.

Suddenly, you think of ways of making sure the audience laughs at that moment. Perhaps the quick cut to the grocery store is all that was needed, to punctuate the laugh. You can use this engagement concept as a tool to figure out when your hero's journey should be shown on screen. You can cue the audience to certain emotions as they watch the events unfold. Just add the phrase "and the audience connects with their emotional reaction through…" to your plot point to help you find a solution.

EMOTIONAL INGREDIENTS

"My wound is geography."

— PAT CONROY, novelist

As filmmakers, we have one thing that no other performance art has — our stories can move freely between wide expanses in geography. This movement naturally provokes emotion. It is essential that we use this to our advantage.

Emotion of Walking Away

Leaving something behind can bring about a swell of emotion within some people. Perhaps you recall how you felt the final time you walked away from high school, college, or a job. As your feet took you away from the building, you may have felt an up-swell of loss, a sense of eerie calm, or even relief that it was finally over. Or that final time you drove away from an old house you spent happy years in — it always makes my eyes tear up and my stomach sink. Visiting a grave of a lost loved one will always do it. But interestingly, the act of actually standing there is always less emotional than walking away.

If moments like these can be used in your movie, use them! Linger on them, and make the audience feel them.

On the other side of the coin, there are equally high emotions when we are en route to something big. Driving to a job interview can be quite nerve wracking, as can going to meet someone who intimidates you. The closer you get to the destination, the greater your feelings of anxiety.

These are the sorts of emotions that movies are best at. One thing that allows film to stand apart from the stage is its ability to use movement through geography. When we see characters moving through the world, it stirs up our emotions.

That's why the movement of character between your scenes is such an important thing to consider. It's such a grand opportunity to tug at the viewers' emotions. When someone walks away from an argument and gets into their car and screeches off, we feel it. That's drama.

The Actor's Face

Another thing films do well is showing different perspectives of the actor's face. If you've seen Gus Van Sant's long 360-degree shot around Casey Affleck's head in *Gerry*, it's a great example of the infinite number of possible "states" that can be captured of the actor based on camera position. It's literally a palette of artistic possibilities. Directors like Hitchcock, for example, used profile shots to show that a character was hiding something, or a dolly-in to emphasize a reaction.

As shown in Gus Van Sant's Gerry, *moving the camera around the actor is an alternative to making the character move through geography in order to express an emotion.* © 2003 Miramax. All rights reserved.

Movement of camera around the actor's face is a viable alternative to moving a character through geography, if you want the character to remain still.

However, movement of both camera and actor together in a tracking or dolly shot is probably the most common way to follow an emotional reaction.

"In my opinion, the chief requisite for an actor is the ability to do nothing well, which is by no means as easy as it sounds."

— ALFRED HITCHCOCK, director

I discovered something amazing when editing my first feature film. The synergistic combination of music and facial expression is phenomenal. When I tell actors how much can be gained by putting music with a shot of an actor's face doing nothing, they bristle. They don't like the sound of that because actors like to think they are always doing something when the camera is rolling. The truth is, in the context of a story, the actor's expressionless face *doing nothing* can express profound emotion when you add music.

That's why at the end of every scene, I always let the camera roll an extra half minute or so. The actor stays in the moment and keeps going. Everyone gets confused, thinking I forgot to say "cut," but it's always good to have those moments in case you need them at the transition. Sometimes you don't really know how the scenes are going to flow together until you see the edit. It's always good to have those extra moments to work with.

Tension

Emotion evoked from geography goes further than just the reaction to plot events. Tension is a specific type of emotion that is something else entirely and exists only in the viewer. The director imposes tension on the viewer through editing and music.

Tension can be created to pressure the characters further while they are reacting to plot events. Example from Alfred Hitchcock's Psycho. © 1960 Paramount Pictures. All rights reserved.

First of all, there will be tension through every scene created by both the interaction of the actors, the pacing, and the editing. In some cases you'll want to extend this tension into the next scene. In other cases you'll want to relieve the tension at the scene transition.

Tension at the scene transition can be sustained by *not* showing the character in motion and simply cutting to the next scene. In this scenario, you give the viewer the impression that the tension is continuing through a series of scenes. At some point you'll have to relieve it — most likely at the next major plot revelation.

Tension at the scene transition can also be raised by interrupting the movements of the characters on their journey. Their car won't start, or they get pulled over by the police, etc. Hitchcock was a master of this type of tension, and would often interject humorous situations that would delay the character's journey. The humor makes the tension more fun. The viewers are on the edge of their seats and loving it.

If the character is pressured into fear while on the journey, it increases tension. Remember Marion Crane (played by Janet Leigh) in Hitchcock's *Psycho*? While she is on her journey after having just stolen money, a policeman follows her and makes her more and more anxious. As a result it increases tension in the viewer, making us side with her. We really hope she doesn't get caught.

In movies where the hero is reacting against a villain, cross-cutting their separate locations together creates tension. Scene A: the villain does something; Scene B: the hero reacts and does something to retaliate; Scene C: the villain does something else. Tension arises through this editing (see Chapter 7).

TO SHOW IT OR NOT TO SHOW IT

Now that you have a good idea of what the ingredients are, it's time to consider which of your 130-plus scene transitions should actually show the character's journey from one scene to the next.

But wait a minute. If all these journeys are important why not show them all? There's a thing in filmmaking called the Law of Diminishing Returns:

If you repeat a film technique within the same film it will be half as effective as the first time you used it, and its continued repetition will eventually grow annoying to the viewer. In other words: repetition generates fatigue.

The director and editor make this decision at every scene transition: *what to show*, *how to show it*, and *how long to show it*. Perhaps editor and film scholar Roger Crittenden said it best:

"Once a scene has served its purpose it's criminal to hold onto it. However, the very essence of a particular sequence can be contained in the pause at the end, and in any case remember that the initial impact of each subsequent scene is dynamically affected by the last moments of the scene that precedes it."

In other words, when you show the hero on a journey you are artistically and emotionally expressing his character. The choice not to express character at a scene transition is just as important as the choice to do so, because all scene transitions work together. The lack of expression in surrounding transitions creates an emphasis on the ones that do express character.

Garden State only has one hero and he appears in every scene, which means every scene junction of the film must feature Andrew exiting Scenes A and entering Scenes B. Zach Braff was smart; by limiting the number of times he showed Andrew's journey, they were more effective because they stood out from the other transitions.

Here's a good rule to follow, the Second Law of Transitions:

Show the character's journey at a scene transition only when it expresses the emotions of the character, or provides an emphasis to something in the plot.

More essentially, if the plot revelation in Scene A was profound enough, lingering on it may be necessary for the viewer to internalize it.

Infinite Possibilities

In order to further demonstrate the process of choosing how much to show, let's take an example from a scene transition in *Garden State*. In this transition Braff doesn't show the character's journey:

Andrew is sitting on the couch at his friend's house and looks at the clock. He realizes he is late for a doctor appointment, rushes out of Scene A and immediately appears in Scene B in the

waiting room of the doctor's office. In the two consecutive shots, we see Braff leave one scene and appear in the next.

There are a multitude of possibilities to fill in this gap with a journey. If you were the director, you might:

- Follow Andrew through the streets in a rushed panic, as he hopes not to miss the doctor appointment.
- Put him back on the motorcycle and show Andrew enjoying the fresh air for the first time.

Garden State, *directed by Zach Braff.* © 2004 Fox Searchlight/Miramax. All rights reserved.

- Pull a Hitchcock, and have the police following him to make sure he's not speeding again. An old lady stops and asks him for directions to delay him.
- Perhaps Andrew has anxiety as he approaches the clinic, feeling his pulse racing as he gets closer and closer.
- Crosscut to a scene with the doctor packing up his things and leaving for lunch. The tension of Andrew's journey increases as he frantically drives. Just as the doctor gets into his car and leaves, Andrew pulls up, missing the appointment.
- Something less elaborate: Cut from Scene A to Andrew nervously walking up to the door in Scene B.

We must assume, however, that Braff made the right choice in that moment. The quick transition works quite well as is. Braff saves showing the journey until, after the scene, the doctor tells him he is fine. Then, when he gets on the motorcycle he has a new lease on life and a new sense of freedom. It's all about saving those journeys for the right moment.

Now let's look at the three times in *Garden State* that Braff did show the journey. I'll emphasize the emotion that is expressed in each one. You'll note that they make a great summary of the movie.

Escaping father's oppression: As his father insults him he walks out, gets on his motorcycle and rides. He is stopped only by a policeman who pulls him over for speeding.

A new lease on life/falling in love: After Andrew's doctor tells him he's healthy after stopping the antidepressants his psychiatrist father had prescribed for him, Andrew rides off on his motorcycle with a new sense of freedom. He stops to give a ride to the girl he met in the waiting room. They ride together, falling in love.

Seeing the past through new eyes: As his friend tells him he's going on a treasure hunt, they all ride once again through the streets of his hometown. This time he sees it from a new perspective, appreciating it in a new way. It's a sense of renewal.

These are the only times that Andrew's journeys on his motorcycle are emphasized in the movie. Clearly he has been riding this bike around a lot more off-screen, but we never get to see it — because we don't need to. If we had seen him riding, these three special moments would mean less.

IF IT'S NOT IN THE SCRIPT

"First, find out what your hero wants, then just follow him!"

— RAY BRADBURY, author

Just like in the preceding example, there may be a moment in your script that you feel needs a journey that isn't there. If you're the writer, it's time to add it. If you're the director, you'll find that this isn't always going to be in the script and may not be implied, which means you'll have to learn to feel when it's missing. Directors must use intuition to anticipate those special moments they think the audience will need to bond with a character.

It's all about the audience. Take this example from a script I directed. This scene is a flashback, so there is no real journey into the next scene. But it's the only time we see the hero, Oliver, reacting to his father's death — something he's been avoiding up until now. Oliver is a doctor in the emergency room as his father is dying on the operating table. As written, this scene is about the lack of emotion from Oliver in this moment. But there's something missing:

```
INT. FLORIDA HOSPITAL - EMERGENCY ROOM - DAY

Oliver makes a move like he's going to resume chest
compressions, but stops suddenly. He knows it's a lost
cause. He breathes normally, calm as ever. No reaction
to his father's death. Only focused on his duty.
```

```
                         OLIVER
               Okay, time of death...

Oliver looks over to a mounted clock, but hesitates to
speak, realizes his lack of a reaction.

The other doctors stare at him with soft eyes. Then con-
fusion sets in. They expected Oliver to do something.
Maybe yell or scream or cry. Something.

Beat. Nothing happens.

Oliver is unfazed by their perplexed expressions. He
simply looks at his father, then stares back at the doc-
tors. There's not a bead of sweat or any evidence on
Oliver's face that suggests a terrible tragedy has just
occurred. He is expressionless, emotionless. How could
this be?
```

This scene is a factual account of what happens, and it's true to Oliver's character. It emphasizes his cold reaction to what has just happened. But what about the audience? Scenes just don't ring true if there isn't some chance for the audience to feel something.

As director I decided that we needed to show Oliver walking away from this scene, in a long traveling shot out of the room and down the hallway. His act of walking away from this tragic scene will strike a chord in the audience, even if he seems to have no emotion on his face. As the viewer, it allows us to empathize with him and feel his loss for him.

Case in point: The focus of the writer and director are different. As the writer, you're going to be quite brilliant in explaining to us what happens in every scene. As a director you have to take that a step further and bring that to the viewer through dramatic visuals. You've got to find emotion. Putting the character in motion through geography is the easiest way to do that.

DIALOGUE IN MOTION

I've spent this entire chapter saying that you should only show a character's journey between scenes in those key moments of emotional expression. But what if your script has an entire dialogue scene in a car, or while walking?

First and foremost think about why you chose to set the scene in motion. Is there a dramatic reason aside from just having another random location to shoot in? Perhaps the dynamic of the moving environment adds something to the tension of the scene, expresses a character's mental state, or contrasts with it.

But more importantly, the act of stopping and getting out of the car may be the key moment that the scene builds to. In this case it all works inversely. Here, stopping and standing still is the equivalent of the dramatic journey at the end of the scene.

If there is more than one character in the car scene, it's possible that the hero is indeed expressing a reaction to what has happened in the previous scene. But the second character may be completely oblivious to this fact and might serve to annoy and add tension. This is another way of interrupting the hero on his journey.

As you see, the line between scenes and scene transitions is starting to become blurred when it comes to character journeys. Entire scenes may serve to emotionally bridge two surrounding scenes.

Chase Films

Let's say you have a chase film which puts the hero in motion a majority of the time.

Chase films are built almost exclusively on the movement of character through geography. The same principles still apply. Take *The Fugitive* (1993) as an example. Both the rise in plot intensity and the hero's reaction tend to happen as he leaves one location and is en route to another. *The Fugitive* follows this basic construction:

1. Dr. Richard Kimble (the hero, played by Harrison Ford) finds new evidence at Location A that will exonerate him of murder.

2. The team led by Deputy Samuel Gerard (played by Tommy Lee Jones) locates him.

3. Kimble evades capture and continues his search for more evidence.

4. While Kimble is en route to Location B, the team finds the new evidence at Location A.

Each time, Kimble is on his journey to a new location and we learn that the deputy is getting closer to believing he's innocent. It connects the plot information to the viewer by using both emotional dramatics and tension.

Your chase scenes should always be surrounded by two major plot revelations, otherwise the viewer will not be sure why they are watching the chase. The scene before your chase will include a plot revelation that sets the character in motion. The chase scene itself will end on some twist to relieve tension, and then the scene immediately after your chase will be another event which may add insight to the chase, or spawn a second chase scene. In Chapter 7, you'll learn more about how to link various types of transitional scenes together into sequences.

ADDING OTHER CHARACTERS

We've been talking about your hero, but now start thinking about all the other characters in the film. There may be moments when you wish to place emphasis on a supporting character or antagonist rather than staying with the protagonist.

Allegiance Shifts

There are times when you may wish to shift the viewer's allegiance to another character. Scene transitions are your best opportunity to accomplish this somewhat difficult task.
All you have to do is use what you learned in this chapter and apply it to the new character. Allow the viewer to spend time with the new character reacting to something big.

Following a new character through geography has shifted the audience allegiance to the new character in Offing David, *directed by Jeffrey Michael Bays.* © 2008 Borgus Productions/Hark Angel Productions. All rights reserved.

I did this in *Offing David*. Throughout the first half of the film the audience identifies with the two heroes, Adam (played by Richie Harkham) and Matt (Adam J. Yeend), then they shift allegiance to a third character, Richard (Brendan Clearkin).

After Matt gets drunk and yells at Richard, I follow Richard down the stairs reacting to this intensity. I stay on Richard as he says goodbye to party guests and walks out the front door. The camera then follows him out to his car where he sits and watches the house in silence. The next morning he's still in his car waiting, and he follows Adam and Matt as they drive away. I continue to keep the focus on Richard's driving as he pursues them in a highway chase sequence.

By staying on the new character for such an elongated period of time, it comfortably allows the audience to shift their emotional connection from Adam and Matt to Richard.

Hitchcock did this quite cleverly in *Psycho* when he shifts audience allegiance from Marion Crane to Norman Bates (played by Anthony Perkins). He does this by staying on Bates for an elongated period of time, using the same principles. Viewers internalize Bates' reaction to the murder he has just committed and watch him frantically clean up the mess. Soon the audience is on his side, hoping that he'll get away with it.

Villain Gets His Moments Too

We've spent all this time making sure the viewer has these magic moments to connect with the hero. Should we do the same with the bad guy?

Yes. The antagonist (if you have one) in your film should get plenty of attention as well. It's easy to disregard his importance or to trivialize him as simply a plot device to keep the tension up. Some excellent films are remembered for their likable antagonists. By giving the villain a few key scenes of his own to react to what the hero is accomplishing, it makes him that much stronger.

Often times, however, when the antagonist is shown on a journey through geography it is in reverse order. Instead of it being shown at the end of a scene in reaction to plot events, it is often shown at the beginning of a scene in anticipation of plot events. Emperor Palpatine arrives and walks down the ramp and greets his troops at the beginning of a scene in *Star Wars: Return of the Jedi*. Because we don't know who he is or what he's doing, this action gives his entrance that mysterious creepiness we all enjoy. In *Gladiator*, Commodus (played by Joaquin Phoenix) is shown riding in a carriage to the battlefield before we even know who he is. But because he arrives late, after the battle has already been won, immediately we know something's up with him.

Often these antagonist journeys appear at the beginning of scenes, because they are taking actions that the good guys must then react to.

Protagonist vs. Antagonist

If your movie is based upon the interactions between a

protagonist and antagonist, you'll be crosscutting scenes in which the antagonist is in one location, and the protagonist is in another.

Here are some interesting phenomena to note while editing your hero and villain scenes together:

- When cutting from a villain scene to a hero scene, the villain's presence is still felt—as if both men are in the same room. One is being defined by contrast with the other.

- When the hero decides to do something and the director cuts to the villain, we feel as if the villain is reacting, regardless of whether he has learned about what is coming.

- Every reaction from the hero as to what has been dealt upon him triggers our memory of what we saw the villain do in the previous villain scene.

- Tension is created merely through juxtaposition of the two geographic locations — Hero Landscape vs. Villain Landscape.

When they finally do show up in the same scene together, the tension will be even more palpable.

Showing the arrival of a villain can build curiosity about who he is, as in this example from George Lucas' Star Wars: Return of the Jedi. © 1983 Lucasfilm/Twentieth Century-Fox.

Supporting Characters

There is no reason to show the journeys of the supporting cast between scenes unless you need an emphasis on their involvement.

If you cut to a scene beginning with a person that we've never seen before, we assume it's a new character. This emphasis will immediately raise the question as to his relevance to the plot and whether his allegiance is to the hero or the villain.

Let's say that you suddenly start following your supporting female character as she walks down the street and puts a letter into a mailbox. Because we already instinctively know she's not the hero, it piques our interest as to what she's doing. That letter must be significant. Or she must be working for the villain!

Often it is useful to end a scene with a reaction shot of one of these supporting characters in order to accent something that has just happened without relying so heavily on the reactions of the protagonist in every scene transition. This is another good way for you to minimize the expression of the hero at the transitions in order to place dramatic emphasis on the key times when you do.

GRAB YOUR SCRIPT

Now, figure out where your characters go after each of your scenes. Many of these journeys will occur off-screen and will never be seen by the audience. You may choose to show some of the journeys for a dramatic reason. Here are some questions you should ask yourself to help you make that choice:

- Does the end of all of my scenes include a burst of new plot information that I've released dramatically to the audience? (If a scene doesn't, it may be a transitional scene. See Chapter 7).

- I've located all of the big emotional moments in my script. Have I allowed the audience to follow a character's reaction to each of these big moments, either through camera movement or character movement?

- When I've chosen to show a character in a journey from one place to another, is there an emotion being expressed? Can I create a transport scene from this?

- Can I evoke the emotions of walking away from something, or evoke anxiety traveling toward something?

- Do I spend enough time with my villain and his or her emotional reactions/journeys?

- Are there better ways I can use my supporting characters to reveal plot clues, create tension, or react to events?

CHAPTER FIVE

EMOTIONAL EBB: SCENERY AND RELIEF

"People have forgotten how to tell a story. Stories don't have a middle or an end anymore. They usually have a beginning that never stops beginning."

— STEVEN SPIELBERG, director

So far our attention has been focused toward the end of your scene; now we'll move to the beginning of the next scene. After something big has just happened, we may or may not have seen the hero react, but because of the filmmaker's skill we've been absorbed into the emotion of the moment.

As this brand new scene begins, things will calm down a bit. It's the emotional ebb. Don't confuse the ebb with boredom. Far from it. As you'll see, there are a multitude of things going on during the ebb.

The audience now has a chance to think about the bigger picture, processing what just happened and how it fits in to the overarching story puzzle. They'll also be lured into the moods and the attitudes that flavor the new scene.

This chapter may seem backwards at first, because I'm telling you things that contradict common filmmaking sense. I'll be telling you to dissipate tension in your film and stop conveying the plot. That all sounds scary and dangerous, so I'll walk you through it.

To Writers: I think this is probably considered non-traditional territory for the screenwriter. Establishing shots are generally not written into every scene of your script. However, key moments of downtime should be considered as you're writing. Hopefully this chapter will help inspire you to find clever ways to accomplish it.

To Directors: You're going to have people telling you from all directions that the pace has to stay fast and crisp. They will tell you that any pause or downtime is going to put the viewer to sleep and cause them to stop watching. This chapter proves them wrong. There are key times to incorporate downtime into your film. The trick is in making your audience unaware of it.

To Editors: As you probably know, scene rhythm is the bread and butter of the editor. It's your job to point out to your director that some downtime should be considered from a key scene to another. Often your director will be thinking of each scene separately, not thinking as much about how they flow together until he sees what you've pieced together. Then all the sudden they will feel that something is wrong in the flow, and you'll be there to help them through it. They rely on editors like you to show them a new perspective. Scenery is easy to put off until last. You should make sure that you either have stock footage to throw into your edit to test ideas, or press the camera crew and director to shoot plenty of it early.

GIVE THEM A BREAK

Movies cannot consist of non-stop tension. If you don't find a way to build relief and pauses into your feature-length film, your audience will be bored and annoyed. This effect is called sensory fatigue.

I once saw a film that really annoyed me (which I won't mention by name) because it never gave the audience a break. The hero was in every scene and constantly in motion, franti-cally trying to fix the situation he was in. The editing of this film was very quick and the camera always shaky. At no point in this film did we ever see a still shot, wide scenery shot, or a shot that stayed on the screen longer than a few seconds. We never got to spend time away from the hero to visit the antagonist, or take time out for subplots and supporting characters. Not once did we get to see any real emotional transformation on the actor's face — he played one emotion throughout the entire film. For 90 minutes we sat there in a state of intensity, focused only on one simple person and the chaotic things that kept happening to him until finally he fell from a tall building and the movie ended.

By the end of the film, I was exhausted, annoyed, and I didn't care. Granted, it's a very cool film, packed with action, but this "always-on" style doesn't work as a serious storytelling vehicle in a movie theater. It might work on commercial television, because then at least you've got commercial breaks. Most likely, this film was designed for the DVD viewer, which could press pause anytime. But that's lazy.

To be fair, this film did everything that they teach in editing class — keep the edit tight, maintain constant conflict, keep the momentum going. But it's missing something. It's missing an opportunity to draw the audience deeper into the story world. If you suspect your film suffers from this problem of sensory fatigue — keep reading. There are clever ways you can take a high-tension film and give the audience breaks without them re-alizing it. Breaks from the tension make those intense moments feel stronger.

We have been accustomed to story breaks for thousands of years. With the stage everyone accepts the curtain pull, the darkened lights, and the music accompaniment to the scene changes. One scene ends, the set changes while the audience waits, and then a new scene begins. Theater also traditionally includes an intermission — a major pause to reflect more than half-way through the story. And in radio and television we have grown up with the commercial breaks. These breaks give us a pause to relax, think about other things, re-gather the senses, and prepare for the next sequence.

Feature films are unique in their ability to capture an audience's full attention in a darkened room for two hours or more with no obvious breaks. Gone are the days when epic features had an intermission.

The feature film storyteller has to find clever ways to fool the audience into thinking there are no breaks, while actually giving them breaks. The movie break is an act of trickery. You create a sense that things are still moving forward while still providing some necessary downtime for mental and emotional processing.

This is where the cinematic ebb comes in.

THE CINEMATIC EBB

"Space does not move, it is."

— JUHANI PALLASMA, architect

The ebb is a bold move in today's fast-paced cinema world where everyone is hopped up on rapid edits and a frenzy of camera movement. I'm here to tell you that it's okay to include moments of pause in your film. In fact, those moments can be quite delicious if done smartly.

The ebb does two important things:

1. Provides relief from the previous event

2. Plants a new mood for the next event

The ebb usually occurs at the beginning of a scene. It's here that you have to build in some downtime that doesn't seem like downtime.

But how do you do this? What's the ebb made of? You can't just cut to five minutes of black space between scenes. Nor can you incorporate commercial breaks — the audience would protest.

VARIATIONS IN CAMERA PROXIMITY

"You see so many movies... the younger people who are coming from MTV or who are coming from commercials and there's no sense of film grammar. There's no real sense of how to tell a story visually. It's just cut, cut, cut, cut, cut, you know, which is pretty easy."

— PETER BOGDANOVICH, director, actor

Scenery in James Cameron's Titanic *gives the viewers a break, but the shot is so beautiful they don't notice the break.*

The simplest and easiest way to provide relief is a wide establishing shot. These have a lot of impact at the beginning of your scene because they have the power to lure your viewer into a new space. It's the idea that something new is about to happen and it's happening in this beautifully chosen setting.

Film is unique in its ability to vary the distance from the subject. The closeness of the camera to the subject is the *Axis of Proximity*. This axis is a scale that ranges between the close-up and the wide shot. It was never possible in theater — each audience member is one constant distance from the stage through the entire play.

The master of camera proximity is Alfred Hitchcock. He saw shot selection as a symphony in which choices of varied intensity play on the audience's emotions. Any time he wanted the audience to feel something, he would either go close or wide. If he wanted to surprise you, he would cut from wide to close.

In his film *North by Northwest*, he began a scene with a wide

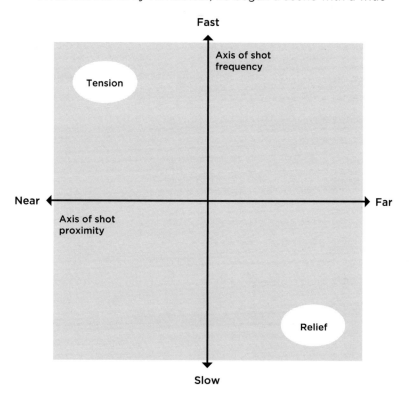

Tension and relief can be attained through combinations of editing and shot selection.

establishing shot of flat farmland. The opening shot is devoid of content, only a highway in which a bus rolls to a stop and lets the hero (played by Cary Grant) off. This shot is held on the screen for 53 seconds. Before this, we've been on a long train ride and a suspenseful chase through a crowded train station. The serenity of this scene not only provides relief, but the stark change in location sparks curiosity.

A wide shot in Alfred Hitchcock's North by Northwest *lasting nearly one minute provides relief while simultaneously prompting curiosity.*

In feature films, the audience can get fatigued by too much time spent close-up on people's faces. It wears thin after a while. A close-up shot, especially of an actor's face, will naturally feel intense, regardless of what is happening in the scene. That close proximity carries with it an inborn sense of intimacy or even discomfort. It comes from the personal space we keep around ourselves in real life. Some people we feel more comfortable being in close proximity with than others. In cinematic story-telling this can be used to your advantage (making the audience feel weird about a bad guy, good about a love interest, etc.) Breaking it by going wide will provide the necessary contrast.

On the other hand, Hitchcock was equally skilled at beginning scenes with close-ups on objects. He would allow the camera to pan a room looking for clues to tell the story visually. Close-ups on scenery objects provide relief because they take time away from the actors.

Starting a scene close on an object can also provide relief. This example is from the Coen Brothers' Miller's Crossing.

A good film will vary along the Axis of Proximity throughout, usually staying somewhere in the middle and then going close or wide during moments of emotion. During the transitions are your best moments to go extreme along the axis — wide or close. If your previous event has just been close-up, a wide shot will naturally give some relief. Close-to-close will maintain tension.

Along with this Axis of Proximity is another axis called the Axis of Frequency. This axis ranges from quick edits to shots held longer on the screen. Tension can be relieved by holding a wide shot on the screen for a while, especially if it follows a lot of quick edits. This axis is discussed more in Chapter 8. Together, manipulating these two axes can provide relief at the beginning of your scene. Tension is maintained by staying close and quick and relieved by staying wide and long.

THE AUDIENCE THINKING AND FEELING

"So much of literary sci-fi is about creating worlds that are rich and detailed and make sense at a social level. We'll create a world for people and then later present a narrative in that world."

— JAMES CAMERON, director

Every scene begins with a process of discovery. Someone has shaken the Etch A Sketch, reset the hour-glass, and given you an entirely new scene to explore.

Mission to Mars, *directed by Brian De Palma.* © 2000 Buena Vista Pictures. All rights reserved.

Think of your story as a journey to Mars. When your space probe lands, the first thing people will expect to see are landscape shots surrounding the landing sight. It's their first glimpse of the new world. Once they're satisfied, then they'll be prepared to look at the detailed rocks up close.

When your scene opens, the viewer first determines which characters are in the scene, where they are in relation to each other and where they are placed in the setting. Instantaneously, the viewer compares this to how the characters were in the previous scene. Questions are provoked such as: have the characters changed since the previous scene? If they're not the same characters, what happened to the others?

If no characters are visible, the viewer will automatically anticipate their arrival. A sense of forward-moving suspense can be generated surrounding the search for these missing characters. The viewer becomes eager to find out what will happen in this new setting. The new scenery becomes a vehicle for introducing a gradual build-up of drama, from the simple to the complex. Gradually the drama builds in the setting like a slow drip that grows to a gushing tsunami.

Hitchcock would often begin scenes with the camera panning a room, looking for plot. Either he would roam through a crowd and then start following one of the characters, or he would zoom into a random window and reveal a story inside. Once inside, his wandering camera would search for clues of a story — an open suitcase, an envelope full of money, a woman packing her bags. This is how he allowed the viewers to feel like they were a part of uncovering the story. It plays on their sense of voyeurism.

Stop Telling the Plot

"Modern-day cinema takes the form of a sermon. You don't get to think, you only get to receive information."

— GUS VAN SANT, director

Viewers' attention at the beginning of a scene is, however, distracted. Most of their mental energy is going toward thinking about what happened in the previous scene and making connections in their minds with the bigger plot. Some questions have been answered and new ones have been raised.

Because of all of this mental activity, the viewer needs time to process without being bombarded with new plot information.

The first thing you must do during the ebb is to stop telling the plot. Don't give them any vital information. They'll miss it. Lack of plot information at the beginning of a scene is essential in creating downtime for the audience to think. What's left in that space is the story context and the underlying mood of your film.

The choices you make in putting your ebb on the screen will rise out of that context and mood. Both affect how the audience is feeling and thinking.

Context and Perspective

When the viewer reaches the end of your film, it's as if he has climbed to a mountain peak and can see everything at once. That's *context*. The context is never fully realized until the final

moments of the film. It is that point when the viewer has fully reached a transcendental vantage point and has figured it all out.

Throughout the film, this contextual viewpoint is constantly growing and changing as the viewers' perspective changes. The higher on the mountain peak they get, the more they see.

As the storyteller, you can manipulate this viewpoint by adjusting the context. That's what storytelling is.

A perfect example of the power of context involves a scene from *Downfall* (2004) where Hitler receives bad news and becomes abusive toward his staff. On YouTube, people have created some brilliant parodies of this scene, simply by changing its context: Hitler reacts to the new iPhone, to the new flavor of Vegemite, to finding out there is no Santa Claus, etc. The exact same scene plays out, but with different context, creating Internet hilarity.

By changing context, drama becomes comedy, boredom becomes suspense. Hitchcock would create suspense in his scenes by using his bomb theory. As an example, show a bomb under the table while the scene plays out with a casual conversation between friends. The characters are all unaware of the bomb, but since our context has been manipulated, it becomes gripping. We want to warn the characters about the bomb, but we can't. Thus, a helpless audience is manipulated by context.

Here are some ways context serves to clarify the meaning of a specific moment:

1. An event is preceded by other events which clarify its meaning. Without the contextual events, the moment lacks a purpose.

2. Setting and atmosphere clarify the meaning of an event. Removed from these contextual clues, the meaning is left to the imagination and may not be as clear to all viewers.

3. The storyteller's attitude and style clarify the meaning of an event. If the intent is clearly comical, the viewer will perceive the event much differently than something with a serious tone.

4. The viewer's own experience and culture clarifies the meaning of an event. Our perception of an event is colored by everything that has happened to us before and our exposure to cultural iconography.

In other words, *cinematic context* creates the foundation for the forthcoming content. It orients us all into the same state of mind so that we can experience the upcoming events in the same way. When you decide to place scenery at the beginning of a scene, you are opening a doorway to this wonderful wilderness of context.

The Ripple Effect

The context of your film is constantly changing. From the opening scene through every event that transpires to the final scene, the context for the viewer grows and changes through time.

Each event affects the next. This is called the *ripple effect*.

"The story is like a river and if you dared to set sail on it,
and if you trusted the river,
then the boat would be carried along toward something magical."

— WIM WENDERS, director

The ripple effect is a temporal process by which any moment within a film is defined by everything that has happened before it, and subsequently defines moments that follow. The result is a flowing process which generally moves in one direction.

It is of great importance to filmmakers because it effects every creative decision on an emotional level. The feeling of a sequence is profoundly tainted by one small change made before it.

"I think film has that power because, unlike most other art forms,
it uses time as a part of its process...You start somewhere,
and then, note by note, you slowly build up
until you reach a particular note that creates a strong emotion.
But it works only because of all the notes that came before it."

—DAVID LYNCH, director

The result is that by changing one scene you change the others.

CONNECTING TO AUDIENCE FEELING

By adding emotion to that flowing story context, you create a story world filled with feelings, attitudes, and intents. These things all surface during the ebb at the beginning of a scene, because it's a moment where there is a lack of plot information. As a result, the audience experiences a process that I call the *contemplation*.

Contemplation = Context + Mood

The contemplation is what the audience experiences as a result of combining the flowing context with moods. This is the moment where they stop to ponder what has happened thus far and speculate on what is coming. The contemplation is dominant primarily at the beginning of scenes. It is like the calm water the surfer floats on when he's waiting for the next wave to come in.

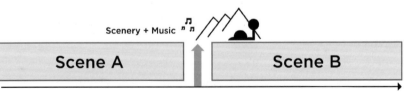

Contemplation (Context + Mood)

As you might suspect, these contextual moods are generated on screen with scenery and music. To simplify it into an easy definition, the contemplation is:

A flowing river of emotionally tinted story context expressed through scenery and music.

The key is that the audience's emotions associated with the contemplation are different than the emotions associated with the hero reacting to events. In the last chapter we called this emotional peak the engagement. The engagement is the strong visceral reaction we get with an increase in plot information at the end of a scene. The contemplation is the opposite — it is the emotion felt with the lack of plot information at the beginning of the next scene.

The two work together. Engagement gradually becomes contemplation during the scene transition, and then the contemplation gradually builds into a new engagement through the next scene.

These two mental states are an overall dueling process by which the viewer interacts with a film. On one hand, the viewer is processing new events as they happen in real time, and on the other hand, the viewer is piecing together a bigger puzzle in his mind.

But at which moments in your film should you make the audience experience this contemplation? Not all scenes should be created equal. Here's an exercise to help you decide whether your scene needs scenery and music.

Let's say the overall story of your next scene is:

Aunt Bell makes tea.

What do you want the audience to feel? What mood and context do you want them to start with before this scene plays out? Let's add the contextual mood component to this scene. Thus we can take our story about Aunt Bell and add more emotional information for the contemplation.

By adding contextual mood, the overall contemplation for this scene becomes:

Aunt Bell comically makes tea on a sunny day in California.

Now, have you prepared the audience with the right kind of mood in order for them to laugh at Aunt Bell's comedy? Perhaps previous scenes have already done this job. You might not need to add any scenery or music to your scene.

Or, you could change the entire story simply by manipulating the contemplation. Let's say you've decided to change the emotion of Aunt Bell's tea-making adventure:

Aunt Bell sadly makes tea on a snowy day in Maine.

It's a different story, all because of the contemplation. You can use this contemplation concept when you're figuring out when to use scenery and music at your scene transitions. The key question is: What does my audience need to feel as this scene plays out? You cue the audience to certain moods and context before they watch the events unfold.

Relationship Between Moods

If your film contains just one mood throughout, you may want to take a second look. Shifting varieties of moods make your movie more interesting. See more about this in Chapter 7.

With the ripple effect, moods become highly interconnected. One mood grows out of another mood. Scene transitions are where all this magic takes place, as this is where the juxtaposition occurs and where the change in mood takes place. The changes in moods, or mood shifts, can be sudden or gradual. If you've just finished a scene that is sad, and then shift to a scene that's meant to be comic, you're going to have to find a way to make that shift work. Otherwise the comic scene is going to fall flat. Often the right type of comedy is a brilliant way to recover from a sad scene.

Hitchcock often said that his suspense stories worked best when they rose up out of a comic setting. If you first capture the audience's loyalty through humor and draw them into everyday characters, then you can throw in the drama. Watch any of his films and notice the humorous tone at the beginning.

Two Emotions Working Together

As you can see, there are two types of emotion at the scene transition. Thus far, we've seen them as separate — engagement comes first, and then the contemplation. But it is possible to mix it up. It's not uncommon to see a hero jump into a car and

have her emotional journey, with a combination of scenery shots providing a new mood and context along the way.

Their turbulent combination at scene junctions lie at the foundation of cinematic storytelling because the engagement rises from within emotional moods generated by the contemplation. They have an interdependent relationship. Without the contemplation the engagement has no energy. Both intertwine to propel emotion through the scene junction.

USES OF SCENERY

"The viewer, while reacting to the scene's beauty,
will also be anticipating some action pertaining to the film...
thus again placing the scene into the context."

— EDWARD DMYTRYK, director

Scenery is the on-screen representation of contemplation. It represents the story context and the moods, and helps to shape them and change them at the scene transitions. Scenery can be defined as a cinematic construction of dramatic space in which an event can occur, where the surrounding is of more primary focus within the frame than the characters.

Scenery for Mood

When scenery first appears on the screen, it's an exciting new place. It sets the mood and dramatic stage for the upcoming event. Scenery generally contains no specific plot information, though it certainly can plant the seeds for things that dramatically appear later.

> *"An event is an entirely different story depending on whether it takes place in a bedroom, library, elevator, or gazebo. An event obtains its particular meaning through the time of the day, illumination, weather, and soundscape. In addition, every place has its history and symbolic connotations which merge into an incident."*
>
> — JUHANI PALLASMAA, architect

Now a word about the weather. The movie cliché is that when characters are angry, it storms, and when they are happy, it's sunny. Whether weather does play a role in storytelling is your choice, but it doesn't always have to follow character mood. It may be that you want it to rain just to contrast with the sun in the previous scene. Or the rain might force the characters to do something they normally wouldn't. Or you might want to create an irony by putting a happy scene in gloomy weather.

Hitchcock frequently sought to break the cliché in his genre by not putting suspense into a dark and stormy setting. In *North by Northwest* he placed his hero in a sunny flat field and generated suspense with a crop duster. It's proof that you don't always have to use the settings that are expected. The contrariness of your choices can add to the tension and excitement of the unexpected.

Scenery for Relief

Rhythmically, the expression of scenery is used for relaxation or relief. The absence of scenery propels tension. At every scene transition you have a choice: Relieve this tension or keep it going.

Let's say you have a long scene indoors. By cutting to a wide shot of the outdoors, you immediately provide relief.

Like most films, *Good Will Hunting* (1997), directed by Gus Van Sant, uses scenery. The film features many wide, sweeping aerial shots above the city at the beginning of scenes to paint a context surrounding the protagonist (Matt Damon), who must face the entrapment of his world. This objective scenery — Boston city skylines, the MIT campus — is a means of relief from dramatic tension between scenes.

In one example Damon is shown riding a train as an emotional transition between events, and then Van Sant cuts to aerial shots of Boston without the presence of Damon. Scene B begins as Van Sant shows a baseball stadium, company logos, and traffic below, making up the Boston cityscape. This lack of character and story information brings the viewer away from plot intensity and thus becomes a state of contemplation.

Cityscape shots in Gus Van Sant's Good Will Hunting *don't include the hero and serve as a moment for the audience to process emotion.*

Van Sant's later film *Gerry* (2003) went further in utilizing long protracted pans of the desert lasting many minutes as a transitional device with flowing clouds.

Scenery shot in Gus Van Sant's Gerry.

Scenery to Set the Scale

Wide landscapes and cityscapes can convey a feeling of grandeur, as a comparison of scale toward a small insignificant character.

> *"Extreme long shots in which a small human figure is dominated by the landscape can make the characters seem vulnerable to larger forces beyond their control."*
>
> — MARILYN FABE, film scholar

Ridley Scott's *Gladiator* utilizes landscape to relieve the viewer from heavy dialogue, and in the transition from the African desert to the antagonist's arrival in Rome, Scott uses an

Ridley Scott plays with our sense of scale in a scene transition in Gladiator.

extreme wide shot of the ancient cityscape, with the Colosseum in full view. Tiny birds cue a sense of scale.

In a later transition, Scott ends Scene A with a small model of the Colosseum and a hand reaching in, then cuts to an aerial shot of the real Colosseum to begin Scene B, further manipulating our sense of scale.

An absence of this grandeur and scope can induce a claustrophobic feeling, as is the case in films like Alfred Hitchcock's *Rope* or Stanley Kubrick's *The Shining* (1980). In *The Shining*, Kubrick's intentional omission of windows creates an internal world devoid of the passing of time, and he resorts to on-screen titles to indicate days passing.

OBJECTS, MOTIFS, SYMBOLS

"You can use a close-up shot in a conventional way — to draw attention to something — or you can use it exactly for the opposite, as diversion."

— DAVID CRONENBERG, director

Scene transitions can be a good time to show important objects that a hero is using in the scene, or to plant the seed for something that will later be used dramatically. Perhaps you want to show recurring symbols that hint at your theme or motifs.

Close-ups of objects are another way to set the scene and still provide relief. It is a more subjective construction of establishment scenery. Still providing relief through lack of plot intensity, close-ups create a sense of momentary disorientation for the viewer in order to convey a shift in time and space.

OTHER WAYS OF RELIEF

There are, of course, other ways to provide relief after a tense scene that are less visual. You also have the option of leaving the hero for a while and focusing on other characters.

Subplots

Subplots are a great way to infuse a bit of a break, and yet still provide us with some entertainment value that eventually ties into the bigger picture. They can be fun distractions that provide a counterbalance to the intensity of the plot.

Comic Gags

The giant frog sticking his tongue out and capturing a dinosaur in George Lucas' special edition of *Star Wars* is an example. This is a gag not in the original film, but he decided to add it to provide depth to his new CGI landscapes. It's also funny and provides the viewer with a chuckle during a break in the action.

Throwaway dialogue

We don't really mention dialogue much in this book, aside from the echo line at the end of every scene. This is because most people don't actually need to listen to the dialogue in order to understand what is happening in a good film. Alfred Hitchcock said that dialogue is just the sound that happens to be coming out of the mouths of the actors.

The beginning of every scene is probably the portion where no one is going to be listening to your dialogue. In fact, you may be able to get away with adding dialogue that doesn't really matter to the plot, as a way of providing relief. It's there intentionally to be ignored!

Throwaway dialogue is like scenery in a way. You're counting on the fact that the audience's minds are preoccupied with something else. It's planting a mood and nothing more.

STORYTELLER'S ATTITUDE

Because you've made a connection to your viewers as the storyteller, they will either consciously or subconsciously feel your presence behind the material. It is at the beginning of scenes where audiences are most aware that a storyteller is guiding them.

Who hasn't gone to a Coen Brothers film, for example, without anticipating that these master storytellers are about to thrill again. Audiences love being told stories, and they love getting their imaginations lost in clever and dramatic weaves of plot. They hold a sense of respect for the geniuses behind the scenes who made it all possible.

Directors tend to get more of this attention than the writers, editors, and other creative people behind the scenes. The director is the chief artist who focuses all the story elements into a coherent style and infuses the story with a certain attitude or tone. By the ways in which you plant the context on-screen as the director, the audience knows whether the film is meant to be tongue-in-cheek, dramatic, or serious social commentary.

If you want to distance yourself from this, you can use a fictional character to narrate the film. This narrator carries with him attitudes toward the material that build trust with the viewers. Because the narrator is fictional, the audience feels safe following the storyteller's logic in order to be entertained.

Spike Lee's *Inside Man* (2006) is an example of a lucid narrative presence in which the flawed anti-hero, Dalton (played by Clive Owen), holds the viewer hostage in the opening moments, controlling how much the viewer knows until the film's final moments. In his voice-over, Owen directs the viewer to "pay strict attention to what I say because I choose my words carefully." While this fictional character serves as storyteller, the viewer also knows that director Spike Lee is manipulating events. There is a clear dual presence which makes up the attitude of *Inside Man*.

If you are using a narrator, scene transitions are the most natural place to insert his or her voice. It is during the cinematic ebb that the audience steps back to objectively think about what has happened, and the narrator can help guide that reflection.

GRAB YOUR SCRIPT

Get out your script and give some serious thought to the beginnings of each scene, sequence, and act. Keep in mind that the transitions between sequences and acts will probably be a lot more dependent on relief than individual scenes.
Here are some questions to ask yourself:

- Does my audience have enough downtime to think and process the emotions of what has just happened?

- Have I momentarily stopped revealing plot information in order to allow the audience to have a break?

- Which scenes in my script would benefit most from starting far away from the subject with landscapes? Which would be better off starting with close-ups on objects?

- Which moments in my script could use scenery to set a mood, or show the scale of a setting?

- Are there clever ways I could use comic gags, sub-plots, or throwaway dialogue to provide some relief at the beginning of a scene?

- Who does my audience feel is the storyteller, and how have I planted the storyteller's attitude? Should I use a narrator?

CHAPTER SIX

MUSIC AND TRANSITIONS

*"To me, movies and music go hand in hand. When I'm writing a script,
one of the first things I do is find the music I'm going to play for the opening sequence."*

— QUENTIN TARANTINO, director, screenwriter

Music and scene transitions have a symbiotic relationship. When you think of adding music to your next film, where do you first imagine it? Between the scenes, of course.

When it came time to write this chapter on music, I turned to my music genius for advice: Composer Spike Suradi (www.spikesuradi.tv) frequently writes scores for TV commercials, short films, animations, and features. Together, we've outlined a few theories of music at the scene transitions.

To Writers: At first you might be thinking that writers really have no input into the realm of music. But it is possible to write music into your screenplay as *diegetic material*. (Sound from a source within the fantasy world on the screen, rather than sound from the film's musical score.) Music can be written as part of the settings, especially for a period piece, as can be special lyrics. Perhaps you can sneak a mention of mood into your description, and this will spark the director to add some music. Nonetheless, this chapter might be helpful for you to understand how music comes into the mix.

To Directors: When I directed *Offing David*, the music I had in mind for the film was completely different from the score I ended up with. Music is one of those things that tends to change as the production progresses. You go through many varieties of temp tracks and editing experiments until you decide on what really works best. Having background knowledge of how music and transitions function can help you and your composer decide things early.

To Editors: Many editors and directors like to use temp tracks to help shape the pacing of their edits, before the actual score is written. What you're really doing is bringing out the contemplation (mood and context) to help you orient the visuals and bring them to life. (See chapters 4 and 5.)

Music is an invaluable tool in the art of scene transitions. When it comes time to start laying music into your edit, how will you know what works and what doesn't? Is it just an instinctual feeling? Will you just know it when you hear it? Yes, but...

Here are some things you should know. At the scene transition, music is going to do one or more of these things.

- Build tension into the next scene.
- Dissipate tension from the previous scene.
- Echo the emotions from the previous scene.
- Set a new mood in the next scene.

There might be some other things that you can think of, but we're pretty sure it will always come back to these basic four. We'll explain why. Before we get into music, though, let's discuss something even more important — silence.

SILENCE

"Without silence the composer loses his most effective weapon."

— WILLIAM ALWYN, composer

It is rare to find films today that contain a soundtrack that fills every frame with music. Scoring music for films is an art of ebb and peak, and composers are particularly good at distributing the amount of emotions we can bear to feel at any certain point. The silent parts of a film score are just as preconceived and planned as the richer parts of the soundtrack.

As a result, silence isn't so much the absence of music, but rather a deliberate choice made by the composer or director. It is the white on a canvas of a whole range of vibrant hues and textures. Silence in film scores can be applied and interpreted in different levels of intensities, or "shades."

The primary reason to insert silence is to provide a sense of space and realism.

Silence also acts as a form of rest between scenes, allowing the audience to distance itself from the events, without being reminded of the multitude of information provided. Consequently, this allows a stronger transition where the purpose of the cut is to move to a completely different frame of mind, emotion, and environment.

But most importantly, it is when silence serves as a contrast to other, louder musical cues that we're able to fully appreciate the richness of the entire score.

MECHANICAL USES OF MUSIC

"The sound and music are 50% of the entertainment in a movie."

—GEORGE LUCAS, director

The presence of music in a film is primarily a signifier of transformation to a new state — new scene, new location, new event, new mood, etc. Often it tends to accompany the manipulation of time such as collage, slow-motion, and the initiation of flashbacks. Any time we shift to a new time or place, music helps ease us into the shift.

As a Lubricant

"A painter paints his pictures on canvas.
But musicians paint their pictures on silence."

— LEOPOLD STOKOWSKI, conductor

At its most primal level, music exists at the scene transition in order to cover and hide the technical imperfections of editing. It essentially serves as a lubricant, like oil in an engine, to keep the viewer from breaking down. Too much technical friction can generate fatigue in the viewer. All of the jolts and shocks that have been covered in other chapters can annoy the viewer if overused.

Music brings calmness and relaxation to the shifts, making them fluid, much as a dissolve softens the transition (as discussed in Chapter 8).

And, because music typically begins well before the actual boundary with the next scene, it prepares us for the shift. It allows the event of the previous scene to move forward into the atmosphere of the next. It provides a sense of continuity that allows us to focus on other elements of the storytelling process.

When the pace of the score is synced to the cuts in the edit, this reduces the phenomena of jumpy editing as well. It alleviates the effects of the cuts between scenes that feel like they've ended too soon or too late. Music essentially becomes one with the edit, and any shock cut becomes united with the flow and aesthetic of the transition.

Film music is felt rather than heard literally, in the same way that the audience is never really conscious of the camera's placement or movement.

Propel or Relieve Tension

Through the scene junction the musical tension rises to a peak, and then relaxes at the beginning of Scene B, much like an ocean wave receding from a beach.

Tension in a film is separate from other emotions and moods. It is a specific tightening of anxiety, curiosity, and pacing that keeps the viewer glued to the material. It is created more through the shot selection and the editing than the actual content of the story. At the story level, tension is generated through conflict or contrast within the characters' actions.

At the scene transition, as you've seen throughout this book, the choices you make either relieve that tension or propel it into the next scene.

Relieving tension is like an archer loosening his draw on the bowstring, or like simply exhaling a breath. Storytellers know that the best way to relieve tension is to reveal something new —

a plot twist. This is why the plot revelations occur at the end of the scenes, so the tension built up from within the scene can be released.

But you don't always have to let all of the tension go; just some of it. That's why sometimes you may want to propel tension into the next scene without relieving it. You release a little, then you ramp it up even tighter in a new direction.

Music can help you accomplish either at the scene transition. Some kinds of music can ramp up the tension, and some can release it. You'll know it when you hear it.

TELLING THE STORY WITH MUSIC

"If I weren't a director, I would want to be a film composer."

—STEVEN SPIELBERG, director

In order to get to the business of storytelling, the primary role of music at the scene transition is similar to scenery. Transitional music typically begins before the actual move into the next scene or location. It accompanies a shift in awareness, as the plot changes the audience's perspective.

In other words, a big event has just happened or something juicy has just been revealed to the hero. As a result, the viewer's perspective suddenly shifts to take in that new information — the story *context* and the *mood* changes. Music coincides with this shifting. Music helps to clarify this shift, so that every viewer feels the same way. It enhances their emotional response.

Transformation

Logically it might seem like the music score simply emotes for the hero — that it just tells us whatever the hero is feeling at any given time. But it doesn't really work quite that way.

At the end of Scene A, music first bathes the hero in a new mood so that when he's reacting emotionally to a plot event, the audience can connect in the way that the storyteller wishes. If the music is comic, the audience will feel laughter. If the music is sombre, the audience will feel sorry for the hero. In other words, it doesn't matter what the actual character on the screen is feeling. What matters is how the audience responds emotionally.

The music score echoes what has just happened. It captures the emotions of the event, then transmits it and reshapes it. By experiencing the emotions of the music, we are allowed to connect with the material and feel a certain satisfaction or closure from the event.

Secondly, the music plants the mood of the next scene. If the moods of Scene A and Scene B are different, the music will transform from one to the other. Or, it will use one of the variations of transformation that we will discuss later.

Setting the Mood

Much like scenery, music is one way of expressing dramatic space through mood and attitude. It can call upon the viewer's knowledge of culture to evoke a historical geographic setting and atmosphere, and it can cue a film genre.

In *Psycho*, the old house near the Bates Motel is turned into a haunted house through Bernard Hermann's score. Likewise, the planet in *Alien* (1979) is turned into something more ominous by the mood-setting effect of Jerry Goldsmith's scratchy and howling score.

"Music usually has the role of reinforcing atmosphere and emotions in films, creating forebodings and surprises, strengthening a sense of reality or unreality, and mediating between different events and scenes in order to create a sense of continuity."

— JUHANNI PALLASMAA, film scholar, architect

Adding Context

The music score gives us information about the scene and manipulates our emotions into interpreting a scene in a specific way. It orients us toward a certain context.

Let's say your scene is about a fight between police and terrorists, like in John Woo's *Face/Off* (1997). Even though the content of the scene is a shootout, you can manipulate your audience to an entirely different focus through music. Woo is well known for juxtaposing visuals and music in his works, presenting a technique that allows him to show the similarities or contrasting ideas between his characters in a scene. During an FBI raid of a gang's hideout, the violent shootout between the police and the terrorists is underscored by a touching rendition of "Somewhere Over the Rainbow," playing diegetically via headphones on a child.

There is a clear contrast between the style of music and visuals in this scene, and that creates context. First of all, the audience's perspective is shifted drastically to that of the child. This is a clear shift in perspective from the rest of the action sequences seen in the film so far, as well as the conventional style of the action genre.

This rubs off on how we perceive the other characters in the scene as well — our hero now fights for the child's safety, the FBI team becomes an antagonist for bringing such violence into the scene, and the audience feels sympathy for the gangsters who are trying to protect the child.

These are all assumptions that a viewer makes, thanks to the powerful suggestions provided by the music. We get caught up in the moment. As long as the music has our attention, the scene is believable.

Recurring Themes

Context can also be planted at the beginning of scenes through thematic music tied to characters, such as the shark theme from *Jaws* (1975) and the Emperor's theme in *Star Wars* (1977). The repetition of these themes throughout the films allows the audience to become familiar with them, and connects their minds to previous events.

VARIATIONS OF TRANSFORMATION TACTICS

Imagine that a line is drawn at the precise moment the scene changes. There are four possible permutations on either side of that line when a director, composer, and editor place music within scene transitions.

- Silence to Music
- Music to Silence
- Music to Music
- Silence to Silence

Each has subtle effects on the viewer, and the following sections go into detail on how music works at the transition.

Silence to Music

This is when there is no music at the end of Scene A, and then music kicks in with the introduction of Scene B.

The tactic of applying music after an extended period of silence allows a release of the pent-up emotions accumulated. It primarily works as a form of catharsis, and as a projected afterthought of the previous events. The music, in turn, will retain the context and emotion of the previous scene, summarizing and reiterating the experience of the character's mindset.

In *Gladiator*, Maximus is sent to be executed by the Praetorian Guard after being betrayed by the newly throned Emperor Commodus. There is no music in the majority of this scene, reflecting the protagonist's calm and pragmatic approach to this dire situation. Music in such a scenario would portray a completely different story and insight into the character's mind. Suspenseful music in this scene would deter and spoil the surprise of his eventful escape. Melodramatic music would provide too much depth into the character's mind and distract the audience with too much information.

The cue eventually kicks in after he kills his guards and escapes. The music now brings a feeling of suspense and action to his movements. The score is suddenly reflective of Maximus' train of thought, almost as if the music had been playing inside his mind previously and has now been released for the audience to hear after he's escaped.

Music, in this case, has the ability to maintain the mood of the previous events and carry it forward to the next scene. The pent-up emotions of the character have been let loose in the form of music and we follow this mindset into the subsequent scenes.

Music to Music

This is when music begins at the end of Scene A and then continues through the beginning of Scene B.

This tactic creates a shift in emotion, from bad to worse, good to bad, etc.

As Maximus continues his escape, a few things happen. A guard wounds him, but he finds a horse which he uses to successfully flee from the rest of the unit. This moment thus cues

another transformation, this time *Music to Music*.

With the *Music to Music* transition, a whole array of emotions can be explored with every coming scene. This tactic is commonly applied to scene transitions that are maintaining or intensifying the energy of the film. In this case, Maximus is successfully fleeing the forest with a new strong sense of confidence and determination. The new scene reflects this, incorporating a more forceful variation of the established escape motif.

Music to Silence

This is when music comes up at the end of Scene A, and then stops fairly quickly with the introduction of Scene B.

This tactic provokes the audience to think. Rather than echoing what has happened or the hero's reactions, it creates anticipation toward what is to come. A waiting sensation develops — the feeling that something new is coming.

Likewise, it allows the audience to reflect on the previous scene without being told how to feel. The silence interacts with the audience, giving them the freedom to interpret the events unreservedly.

Silence to Silence

There is no music at all in these scene transitions.

Silence to Silence works similarly to *Music to Music* in maintaining the desired pace and emotion. It is basically an extended period of silence in the transition, so the afterthoughts and mood of the previous scene are neither dissipated nor released.

There are also different variations of these tactics that work very similarly to *Music to Silence/Silence to Music*. Minimalistic scoring can be so subtle and discreet that it provides a soundscape rather than an enrichment of the emotional composition of the scene. It blends into the atmosphere of the scene very well, serving the same basic functions as silence.

USING PRE-RECORDED SONGS

Many filmmakers like to use pre-recorded songs in their movies. "Pre-recorded song" refers to a song that was composed and recorded before the filming of the movie. Any changes made to the edit will be in the visuals, to match the pacing of the song. A pre-recorded song is also made to stand on its own without visual accompaniment.

A film score, on the other hand, is made to precisely match a visual edit already in place, and is not designed foremost to stand on its own as an orchestral performance.

The use of songs at the transitions works in the same way traditional scores do. Songs can also be a way to connect to the audience, by using selections that are catchy or popular for a given time period. By beginning the song just after a major event has occurred, it releases the emotions felt by the hero so that the viewer can feel them. Once the transition to the new scene has transpired, the song is faded down gradually as the next event begins.

Songs are often used over collage sequences (see Chapter 8) such as opening scenes and clips summarizing events. When music is added, the editing becomes a part of the pacing of the song, rather than vice versa.

Period music is a great way to set the atmosphere and mood of a certain era. It can do so in a way that is often superior to a film score.

THE ROLE OF LYRICS

Lyrics in film music serve a function quite similar to that of a narrator. They either speak for a character or comment on what's happening. It brings the viewer out of the story to a more objective stance.

The words are, of course, often poetic. They comment on themes and motifs that are ongoing in the film.

Musically, vocals are essentially the same as instrumentals. They are just one layer of the overall emotional harmonic. Even if the words aren't understood by the audience, their sound brings forward a mood and attitude that otherwise could not be obtained.

Mike Nichols' *The Graduate* (1967) contains a soundtrack with many songs written by Paul Simon and Art Garfunkel.

"The Sound of Silence," for example, is played numerous times in key parts of the film:

> Hello darkness, my old friend,
> I've come to talk with you again,
> Because a vision softly creeping,
> Left its seeds while I was sleeping,
> And the vision that was planted in my brain
> Still remains
> Within the sound of silence.*

Consequently, the lyrics serve as an inner monologue of the title character — Benjamin Braddock, played by Dustin Hoffman — during the scenes in which the music is played. In the opening sequence of the film, the music is played as Benjamin stands on the moving walkway of the airport terminal, staring blankly into the distance in an awkward, robotic fashion. Already we get the impression that the film is about a character who is unaccustomed to his surroundings.

GRAB YOUR SCRIPT

Now go back to your script and start thinking about where the music should go. In order to help you think about which transitions need music, ask yourself these questions:

- Do I want to use music to maintain the tension from this scene and build it even stronger into the next scene?
- Do I want to use music to dissipate tension and provide a calming sense of relief going into the next scene?
- Can my music echo the emotions of the previous scene?
- How do I want my music to plant the moods of the next scene?
- How should I handle this musical transformation from the emotions of one scene into the moods of the next?
- Would any of my transitions benefit from silence?

---

*© 1964, 1992 by Paul Simon Music.

CHAPTER SEVEN

PUZZLING THE SCENES TOGETHER

"A film is — or should be — more like music than like fiction. It should be a progression of moods and feelings. The theme, what's behind the emotion, the meaning, all that comes later."

— STANLEY KUBRICK, director

Imagine a 90-minute song that held one note and never changed! Who would listen? It would most likely induce a headache.

Feature films are long enough that they require patterns of tension and release. You can't get away with full tension for 90 minutes without some sort of break. There have to be ebbs and peaks.

Failure to build downtime into your film will generate sensory fatigue in your audience. They'll get tired of the intensity and their brains will tune out. It would be the equivalent of a song consisting of one note being played continuously for a long period of time — no rhythm, no beat, and no emotional variation.

That means your scenes have to vary in intensity and mood. They have to induce rhythm when placed next to each other. Your scenes, of course, have variety within them, but this chapter will focus on the bigger picture — the way the scenes flow, one after another.

To Writers: The best screenwriters are finely tuned to scene flow. While some might say that rhythm is a director's and editor's game, writers can shape the rhythmic flow of events in their scripts to evoke strong emotions in the minds of their readers. As a writer, it can be easy to start worrying about how many pages a scene should be, or if there's too much dialogue. As you'll see in this chapter, variety and contrast are key. By varying your scene lengths or adding silent scenes between your dialogue scenes, you create a vibrant mix that stirs up emotions in your readers.

To Directors: This is what directors are paid to do. Traditionally, film rhythm comes from instinct, and no one can agree on it. That's why they bring you (the director) in to sort it all out and call it "art." You're probably most familiar with beats within a scene, and the rhythmic editing of shots within that scene. But it's easy to forget how those individual scenes will flow together in sequence. You probably have a vague feeling inside your gut about how your scenes will flow, but it's so easy to procrastinate until the editing room. Planning ahead can help. You may have thought that the establishing shot of the highway wasn't necessary. Oops! It would be nice to have it now that you've seen how two tense scenes go together and are missing some relief. This chapter will help you map out the emotional rhythms in your screenplay, and help you find where the most important transitions should go. Do this before the camera rolls and you'll save time, reduce expenses, and eliminate needless frustration.

To Editors: Rhythm is everything to you. This is what you live and breathe in the dark recesses of the editing studio. Your instinct for timing is most likely inherited from your love of music. It's the instinctual merging of moods that we'll be diving into here. The director is going to need your help in sorting it all out and coming up with possibilities. Let's get started.

TENSION AND RELEASE

A common theme through this book is that scene transitions can either propel tension or release it. Let's review:

Location Choices — by creating contrast between two locations, you create relief. Darkness is relieved by sunrise, chaos is relieved by calm, indoor is relieved by outdoor, etc. Similar locations placed next to each other will therefore inherently maintain tension from the previous scene.

Linking Events — linking scenes through similar objects, themes, characters, or ideas keeps the tension tight. Not linking scenes together generates relief.

Character on the Move — showing a character's geographic journey between locations increases the emotional connection with the viewer. This can provide relief of tension (in a meaningful way, of course). By not showing the character's journey between locations, you propel tension.

The ebb — showing scenery at the beginning of a scene relieves tension, and not showing it increases tension.

Music — some types of music can heighten tension, others can relieve it. Silence can also do both.

There is no right or wrong way to use these elements. As you'll see in this chapter, they are tools you can use to manipulate the overall rhythms and flows of your scenes.

SCENES AND THEIR FLOW

"A film with a satisfying flow of scenes is more successful than a film which, while individual scenes may be well-edited, does not flow together to create a satisfying whole."

— WALTER MURCH, editor

A film is like a river. Everything downstream is affected in some way by everything upstream. When you place scenes together, a flow and rhythm are generated.

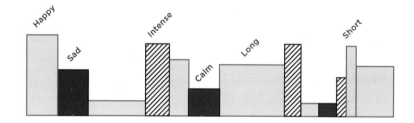

Scenes of various lengths, intensities & moods

Scenes of varying moods, intensities, and other aesthetic properties create the emotional rhythms from which the art of *scene-making* emerges. There are two things to consider in this chapter:

1. How the scenes fit together

2. How the transitions emerge between them

The rhythmic pattern of a film's scene structure is very similar to music. Scenes that flow past one another should build to crescendos and wane to softness, all in a buildup to a big finish and a coda.

The very idea of scenes in film grows out of theater, which has its roots in music. Literature also has its roots in music through poetry. You can't really discuss either without acknowledging the fact that nearly every performance art we have today can be traced back to music in some way.

Not surprising then that your decisions involving scene rhythm are similar to the decisions that composers and musicians make in their craft.

Rhythm on the macro level of a film can be achieved in large part by the way the scenes of various lengths, intensities, and moods are placed together.

What's a Good Length?

The great cinematic guru David Bordwell likes to do statistical research on movies to find trends in editing over the decades. He sampled some films from various time periods and calculated their average length of scenes. He found that before 1960, films averaged around three minutes per scene, with many scenes running longer than three. After 1960, scenes averaged less than three minutes, with many much shorter. In contemporary Hollywood, scene length has shortened even more significantly, with some films averaging about one minute per scene.

Clearly, scenes have gotten shorter over the years, but what does this mean for your film?

When I worked in commercial radio, I used to produce commercials that were written and prepared by the sales team. Clients were buying 30-second commercials and wanted to squeeze in as much content as they could to get their money's worth. I would often get scripts that were easily 60-seconds long that I was expected to read quickly and fit down into 30. The result is something that no human wants to hear — nonstop frantic talking with no pauses whatsoever. Where's the story? Where's the drama? It's all lost in the hurried quest for time-crunching. How do you connect like that with a listener? Truth is: you don't.

When measuring the length of your scenes, don't get caught up in an oppressive rush to keep things short. Focus instead on the feelings that you want to create in your audience. If more time, slower pacing, and more pauses are necessary for the emotions to sink in — allow more time. Any great storyteller will tell you: The key is to create rhythms and variations in your pacing.

LOOKING AT THE SCRIPT

"I love more than anything looking at a movie scene-by-scene and seeing the intention behind it."

— JODIE FOSTER, director, actress

Go through your script and ask yourself these questions about your scenes: *How long are they? How intense are they? What mood are they?* You'll hopefully notice some patterns emerging.

This exercise can be used to locate problems in your inter-scene rhythm by breaking down everything into its parts. I'm not suggesting that you should spend a lot of time mapping out your entire feature film, but this will certainly help with problem areas that you're feeling vague about.

Length of Scenes

Yes, it is possible to create a film in which every scene is exactly the same length. But when it comes to craft, it gives you more options if you can manipulate the flow of a film by simply adjusting the lengths of all the scenes in a rhythmic way.

Most films naturally tend to have shorter and shorter scenes as the film builds to a climax. This is especially true if things are repetitive — the audience can deal with abbreviation to speed things along.

What if we constructed a sequence like this:

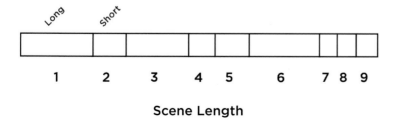

Scene Length

The varied lengths of each scene play a large role in the rhythm of an entire film. Some directors like Jean-Luc Godard would plan out a film's macro rhythm first, deciding how long each sequence would last before adding the content. This top-down approach may be a bit extreme, but it's worth noting.

Length is slightly different from *duration*. Duration is how long the scene feels when watching it in sequence. A long scene can actually feel short and vice versa. Perceived duration also depends on the pace of the surrounding scenes. If you've just gone through a bunch of fast action, a slow scene is going to feel nice and relaxing. If you've just sat through a series of slow scenes, a new slow scene may feel a lot slower.

If a scene is there to reveal character depth, hold it longer than you normally would. When editing, always think of how things feel as a result of what has happened before it. A scene watched in isolation will feel a lot different without the context of what preceded it.

My rule in the editing room: edit long and then cut it back later.

Intensity of Scenes

Generally if a scene is intense, it's going to be fast-moving with a lot of action, conflict, and quick editing. It could also include a scene that is just downright scary and heightens tension.

A series of tense scenes could be followed by a calm scene.

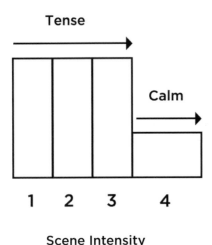

Scene Intensity

A calm scene is generally going to feel more relaxed. A very quiet scene can still be insanely tense. Keep in mind, most scenes are going to start calmer than they end. In this instance we are focusing on the overall intensity of a scene.

By varying calm scenes and tense scenes, you can create a rhythm that keeps the audience entertained. Of course there are going to be various degrees of intensity and calmness as well. It's just like music. There are many notes.

When I was working in radio, our station's music collection had a label on each song to indicate its tempo — up, medium fast, medium, medium slow, or slow. We knew never to switch from a slow song to a fast song without including a medium song in between. It was also our station's policy to play up-beat songs between sports broadcasts, so the sports audience wouldn't get bored waiting for the next game and tune out during a slow ballad.

Before long these rhythms became subconscious. The same can be true for your selection of scenes for your script or film.

Mood of Scenes

Mood is more complicated and this is where you come in as the talented artist. Mood is an overall feeling at the beginning of a scene. It is not what the character feels at the end of a scene; it is what they feel at the beginning, before they react to new events. Reacting to events is a boiling of emotion beyond the mood, and is the basis for transitions. The mood is usually a combination of the reaction to the previous scene and the new mood in the next scene.

A sequence of scenes might look like this:

Scene Mood

In the illustration, the first two scenes are "happy" and "angry." The anger probably happened toward the end of the happy scene, and then was carried forward. What the character feels at the end of a scene carries over to the next scene. The character is a mood connector.

It's a good idea to go through your entire script and at the bottom page of every scene note what mood you think the scene feels like. When you start combining all these patterns together, you literally start conducting a score. Instead of musical notes, you're using scene moods.

Combining Them

Once you have noted the length, intensity, and mood of your scenes, it will help you see the overall rhythms of the film.

A complex sequence might go like this:

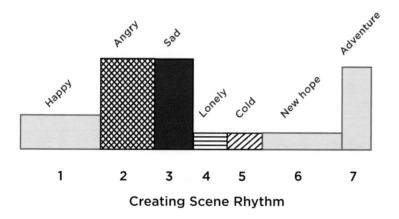

Creating Scene Rhythm

Scene 1: Long, calm, happy
Scene 2: Long, tense, angry
Scene 3: Short, tense, sad
Scene 4: Short, calm, lonely
Scene 5: Short, calm, cold
Scene 6: Long, calm, new hope
Scene 7: Short, tense, new adventure

The combinations are endless.

This exercise helps you see whether you have enough variation in your story. The sample sequence starts out with a long scene with a happy mood where not much happens. Then, we go through many variations until we end the sequence on a positive note filled with tension. If all of these scenes were calm, or they all had the same mood, it might be problematic.

It's literally like the DNA of filmmaking — by arranging just three variables we are able to paint an emotional journey. Granted, this is just a starting point. Once your film comes to life, there will be much more richness to what it has to offer.

This will also help inform your decision at the scene transitions, because it helps determine when establishing shots should create relief, for instance.

DELETED SCENES

It's really only with the advent of the DVD in the last decade that we have, as audiences, been treated to the scenes that were omitted from the final cut.

We often hear stories about how a director demanded to leave scenes in the film but the studio forced them to be cut, or vice versa.

The reason for deleting a scene besides the obvious — that it wasn't good enough — is primarily for emotional flow. It may be because:

1. The actors' performances gave the scene a mood or note that just didn't match the surrounding scenes.

2. The story content is better left unsaid. Rather than spell out to the audience a certain fact, the director may decide that it's more fun to make the audience wonder, and strengthen the impact of another upcoming scene. More on this in Chapter 8.

3. Tension is another reason to cut a scene. Perhaps the scene was dissipating tension that needed to be tight going into the next scene.

What if there's a scene that you like and you just don't want to delete it? Here are some alternatives to using deleted scenes elsewhere in your edit:

1. You could juggle it into a different place in the film — out of intended sequence — and see if the plot still makes sense.

2. You could turn it into a flashback.

3. You could even crosscut it with another scene and increase tension in both.

FRAGMENTATION AND CRESCENDO

Deleting scenes and varying their levels of tension and mood are not the only ways to control the rhythm in your scene flow. Crosscutting slices up scenes and combines them alternately into one sequence. This is called scene fragmentation.

Fragmentation can be a fix for a flow pattern in the editing room. It's a way of cutting scenes into fragments and alternating them in order to generate tension or further cohesion. It has these effects:

1. Connects the events.

2. Generates new tension between them.

3. Creates the sense that scenes are happening at the same time.

4. Gives the viewer an objective vantage point greater than that inherent in each scene alone — from which to discern meaning.

As both events build toward their peaks, a larger crescendo happens at the end of their combined sequence.

The Aronofsky Quintuple Crosscut

Fragmentation can be used to combine more than two scenes together. Director Darren Aronofsky's *Requiem for a Dream* (2000) exemplifies an extreme form of fragmentation through its climax sequence in which five scenes are juxtaposed in rapid succession:

Scene 1: Harry (Jared Leto) is dying in the hospital.

Scene 2: Harry's mother Sara (Ellen Burstyn) is having radical weight loss treatment.

Scene 3: His girlfriend Marion (Jennifer Connelly) is having an affair at a sex party.

Scene 4: The television audience from the show Sara has been watching is cheering on Marion.

Scene 5: Tyrone (Marlon Wayans) is mopping the floor in prison.

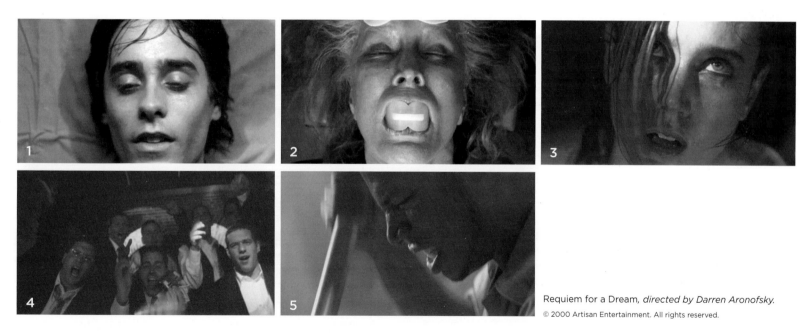

Requiem for a Dream, *directed by Darren Aronofsky.*

These five scenes could be shown separately; however, through tension, Aronofsky's use of fragmentation creates rhythm as the fragments grow increasingly shorter and faster. This also allows a heightened comparative function as parallels between each scene are drawn — in this case, the frenzy of obsession.

The Figgis Tic-Tac-Toe Cut

In his movie *Timecode*, Mike Figgis (director, writer) takes this a step further by splitting the frame into four segments and playing four scenes simultaneously. In this way, the fragmentation occurs within the composition of the frame, rather than by editing the scenes together in temporal succession.

INTENSITY OF TRANSITIONS

Now let's go between the scenes and look deeper into your transitions and their own rhythms. Once you've got your scene blocks in place, the style in which you move between each scene also has rhythmic concerns. As we will see with all choices made at the junctions, it is the degree of intensity of the usage that makes up the true cinematic art.

First and foremost, transitions are the shift of change from one mood/intensity/pace to another. A transition includes the area at the end of Scene A when things begin to change all the way through the beginning of Scene B. Some transitions can stretch from the middle of one scene to the middle of the next. It covers a wide swath, dependent on how gradually the change occurs.

Rhythmically, transitions are the peaks and valleys of your scene rhythm. Your transition can be intense, filled with drama and tension, or it can be more subtle — so subtle that the audience doesn't even feel the scene changing.

Now let's take a look at an earlier example. We've got two scenes. One is "happy" and the other is "angry." In order to shift the audience from happy to angry, what choices should we make at the transition?

First, let's assume that the hero has shifted from happiness to anger, so it is our hero that is going to be angry. To connect with the hero's anger, we want to show his reaction. Since anger is a volatile emotion, we may want to use quick edits and keep things tense at the transition. Perhaps we could use shock cuts as he slams his car door, opens another door, slams that door, opens another, throws his wife's laptop into the street. This quick collage of shock cuts helps the audience feel his anger. As the laptop is flying through the air we could show it in slow motion, to draw out the tension and shift the audience to a more objective mode. Now we've set up the next scene to be angry, transitioning from happiness.

What if, however, we are going from a "sad" scene to a "lonely" scene? Our approach is going to be a bit different in designing the transition here. Let's assume that the hero is sad, and then will feel lonely in the next scene. This time we may want to use very long, drawn-out edits. A dolly shot around his face can depict his change of emotions as he has just learned bad news. We can show every action he takes to leave the house, lingering on it. We show our hero walking down the street in a daze. We can switch to wide, expansive shots of each part of the neighborhood he walks through to show him as a small, insignificant figure in a massive, lonely world. The music swells up and the audience connects with his loneliness. Now we've set up the next scene to be lonely.

You don't want all of your transitions to be the same, otherwise they will grow tiring. Just like your scene blocks should vary in intensity and mood, so too should your transitions.

Here are some variations to consider in your transitions:

Transitions

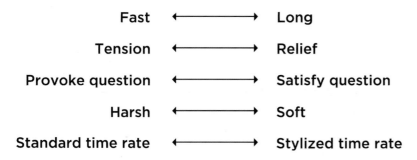

Fast	←——→	Long
Tension	←——→	Relief
Provoke question	←——→	Satisfy question
Harsh	←——→	Soft
Standard time rate	←——→	Stylized time rate

Fast/Long — the period of change at the scene transition can either occur very abruptly or it can happen over a gradual amount of time.

Tension/Relief — as mentioned at the beginning of this chapter, a transition either propels tension or relieves it.

Provoke Question/Satisfy Question — Plot points always reside within the realm of the transition. The transition plants questions in the viewer's head and then either immediately answers them at the beginning of the next scene or keeps them unanswered for a later revelation at another scene transition.

Harsh/Soft — the transition will either be aesthetically bold, like a shift from day to night, or it may be so soft that it isn't noticed.

Standard Time Rate/Stylized Time Rate — when things are changing at the scene transition, you can speed up or slow down the frame rate, or keep it normal.

All of these variations can be adjusted in order to precisely tailor moods to your liking.

As you can see, overall rhythms play into your choices at the transitions. Let's say your script has a series of scene transitions in a sequence like this:

Scene 1: Calm
Transition 1: Relief, Long, Provoke a Question, Soft, Standard Time

Scene 2: Calm

Transition 2: Tension, Fast, Provoke a Question, Soft, Standard Time

Scene 3: Tense

Transition 3: Relief, Fast, Answer a Question, Harsh, Faster Time Rate

Scene 4: Tense

Transition 4: Tension, Fast, Provoke a Question, Harsh, Fast Time Rate

Scene 5: Tense

Transition 5: Relief, Long, Provoke a Question, Soft, Slow Motion mixed with Fast

Scene 6: Calm

With this example, you can see how patterns and rhythms can be formed within the transitions as your scenes flow past. This is craft used to create art. The more you pick up on this craft, the greater you'll be able to manipulate your audiences to the desired effect, just as a composer does through his symphony. You could rhythmically build to something more profound at the end of the sequence.

Notice in the example how we've alternated tension and relief. Even with this, you can adjust the degree of tension, gradually building it toward a greater relief in Transition 5. Also note how we've spent more time with the transitions at the beginning and end of the sequence. Presumably there is more story drama to tell in these bigger sequence transitions. We don't linger on the transitions in between.

Depending on the plot, sometimes you want to get the audience thinking and raise a question in their minds. Sometimes you want to satisfy that curiosity with an answer. The transitions are the best time to do either.

We've also increasingly manipulated time rate as the sequence builds. In Transition 5 we've fully mixed slow motion and fast motion as a stylistic way of getting into the characters' emotions but remaining objective.

So you can see, if all of your scenes and transition styles in your movie are the same, your audience is in for a boring ride. Now go out there and make rhythm!

TYPES OF TRANSITIONAL SCENES

All scenes contribute to transitions, but not all scenes are created equal. Beyond the basic scene structure, there are special scenes that serve as transitions linking other scenes. These scene types are the major building blocks of your film. They can either include the hero or the villain.

Event

The most basic and common form of scene is the event. Placing two event scenes together creates a standard transition.

In an event scene, a setting is staged and then something happens and the characters react. These reactions cause them to make choices which lead to the next event scene.

Transport

When a hero is in motion from one event scene to another, and the filmmaker has decided to show this journey on-screen, the result is the *transport* scene. This scene serves as a transitional scene between two event scenes. Chase films have lots of these.

Collage

Smaller mini-scenes or shots combined in order to show the passage of time, or to quickly summarize events, are classified here as a *collage* scene. This type of scene is a transitional scene which bridges two bigger event scenes. They have the effect of taking the viewer out of the story and into a more objective stance. Note: transports and collages can be combined into a hybrid scene in which the character is in motion through geography and the director switches to objective mode through collage.

In Medias Res

This is a scene that defies the logic of the basic event, by throwing you into a scene already in progress. *In medias res* is a common transitional scene to open a film by bringing the viewers into the story through its sudden shock value and then making them frantically guess how to piece together the meaning of events. It is so different from the standard scene that I mention it here as a separate classification, because it is indeed a transitional tactic on its own.

Subplot

The *subplot* scene contains supporting characters and follows a story not directly connected to the main plot. It is a transitional scene that allows the audience to take a break from the main action and find out story information behind the hero's back.

Every film has a major plot surrounding a hero, usually along with a villain. Feature films are long enough that they can include minor characters which are somehow tied to the hero or villain. These minor characters make up the subplots and often have scenes of their own.

Subplot scenes can be used in your puzzle match-up as a way to rest, to take a break from the main characters. Subplot scenes may just be there to add comic relief in the midst of a tense sequence, or their actions may also affect the main story indirectly. They may also plant clues and generate a tug of curiosity in the audience by their mere presence.

The audience, seeing characters that don't seem to fit, will automatically be prompted to try to weave in meaning. Let the audience do the work in making sense of it all. Their appreciation will be heightened, although they won't be aware of the reason. The reason they'll remember: You made a subplot scene.

Caboose

This is another special scene that defies the basic construction. The *caboose* scene is a transitional scene that trails off into an ebb without any peaking of plot intensity. It is designed to allow the viewer to let go and come back into reality. It is usually the last scene of a film.

BRIDGING THEM ALL TOGETHER

"It's all just one film to me. Just different chapters."

— ROBERT ALTMAN, director

In this chapter we've added some shape to the craft, but there are no easy answers. When it comes right down to it, a filmmaker must do what feels right in the moment.

Your film will string together various types of scenes with different moods, lengths, and intensities. The transitions between them will emerge and you'll have to decide what to leave in and what to hide during the shift from one scene to another. The next chapter will talk more about this in depth.

GRAB YOUR SCRIPT

Think about your film and how the flow of your many scenes create rhythm. Here are some basic questions to consider:

- Do my scenes vary in length, intensity, and mood?
- Can any two or three of my scenes be combined into a crosscut sequence?
- Can I create a flowchart of my film from my various types of scenes (event, transport, caboose, etc.)?

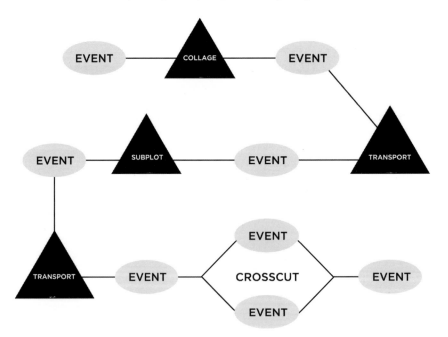

CHAPTER EIGHT

THE TIME MACHINE

"Cinema is a matter of what's in the frame and what's out."

— MARTIN SCORSESE, director

To become a true master of scene transitions you must come to know a tactic which has been used by storytellers for centuries — telling a story through omission.

What you leave out of the story is equally as important as what you leave in. It's these gaps of missing information that bring the story to life. In literature, this is a process known as ellipses. Psychologists call it the Gestalt Theory. Alfred Hitchcock said it best: "Drama is life with the dull bits cut out."

This chapter will focus on the material that isn't in your film and how it shapes what remains on the screen. Knowing how to balance the withholding of information versus revealing it is the hallmark of a great storyteller.

To Writers: Probably the safest thing a writer can do is write too much material and too many scenes. As long as the scenes are rock solid and have a meaningful purpose at the writing stage, if in doubt, leave them in. The reason I say this is because by the time your material gets to the editing room lots of cuts are going to be made. Entire scenes and sequences will be removed or reduced substantially. That doesn't mean you should leave badly written scenes in your script. You still want people to read it. Leave it to everyone else to make the cuts and don't get too upset when they do.

To Directors: Deciding what to cut and what to leave is a huge decision. This chapter may help you wade through the basics to help ease that pain. We will also go through some basic visual tactics to help stylize the transitions between scenes to mask the holes left by the things you cut out. As always, the primary concern for you is: What will the audience think and feel?

To Editors: This is your territory. My advice to editors is to always start with the longest possible edit that you can reasonably create, and then start whittling it down. In your first assembly edit, stretch all scenes as long as they can go, with as many raw pauses and moments as humanly possible, and try to leave all scenes intact. Then go through and see what can be abbreviated, and put Band-Aids on the sutures. Once you and the director have agreed on the shortened edit, and after you've been bored by the material sufficiently, leave it a few days and then go back to watch that first long edit. Can some things go back in? It's a delicate dance.

STORYTELLING IS ABBREVIATION

As a filmmaker, you have the keys to the time machine. You can take us any place and any time at the flip of a switch, click of a mouse, or tap of a finger. As viewers, we absolutely love the prospect of this ride through time. That's why we plunked down the cash and settled into the cinema seat.

But your audience has some rules: It only wants to see the important parts. Show us the highlights — all the dramatic parts, the parts that reveal character, the parts that make us feel something about ourselves. Pique our curiosity but, if you don't mind, please wrap it up within two hours because we're busy people! Unless you're James Cameron, we don't want to sit through your four-hour epic.

Alfred Hitchcock used to tell a joke about this: "The length of a film should be directly related to the endurance of the human bladder." This is a coy remark about the intensity of his suspense techniques, but he was also being serious about the fact that you don't want your audience getting up to use the restroom in the middle of your film.

Filmmaking is like making a sculpture. Only when the extraneous material has been removed can the final form be seen. The remaining material reveals the shapes and patterns that, hopefully, people will recognize. You must remove all the parts that don't belong and what's left is your story.

Documentary filmmakers know this all too well. Trolling through hours and hours of raw footage, finding only the good moments, trimming them all down to a succinct shape — it's a process that creates gripping drama out of boring reality. Film is, at its best, abbreviation.

The Gestalt

"Usually when I read something, first of all I'm looking for the story and then when I reread it, I'm sort of checking every part of it to see if every scene is necessary. You imagine yourself watching the movie, to see whether or not you're losing the through-line of the story."

—GUS VAN SANT, director, screenwriter

Missing information prompts us to fill in the blanks with our imaginations. Because our minds have done the work, we internalize the information we created on an emotional level. We connect with the material because we feel involved with the creative process.

Gestalt is the magic that happens when the brain sees something that isn't really all there but is perceived because the surrounding elements suggest it. The little black blotches in this drawing have been arranged in just the right way to suggest an object. Would a photograph of a giraffe carry with it the same emotion as this blotch drawing? Probably not, because at least 50% of this giraffe exists entirely in your mind.

Imagine that each of these black blotches are the scenes in your film and the white space is your story.

When you are sitting in the editing room working on the final edit, polishing the final draft of your screenplay, or even trimming the budget, you should ask yourself about each scene: *Would this scene be more powerful if we left it out?* Often times the answer is surprising. The human mind has an amazing ability to add missing details.

> *"Art thrives on restrictions and on things left out.*
> *It is in every case the imaginative participation*
> *of the reader, the viewer, the auditor,*
> *that completes the circle to make it art."*
>
> — NICHOLAS MEYER, director, author

The obvious example of Gestalt in filmmaking is the all-too-familiar scene in which a romantic couple is sitting by the fireplace and the camera pans away. Cut to the next morning. What happened there is left to our imagination.

By removing a chunk of time, you prompt the audience to think. You force the audience to wonder what must have happened. This active audience is suddenly engaged and doing the work for you. Not only does the human mind enjoy this kind of puzzle, it demands it. This provocation of the viewers to search for a missing piece in the puzzle fully engages them in the story at every scene transition. If you spell everything out for us and show everything, we get bored. The folks over at C-SPAN are great, but they'll never win an Emmy for gripping drama.

With rare exceptions, all films use Gestalt, and as such there are an infinite number of ways to provoke the viewers' imagination through omission. It's also great for the budget!

Shorten the Transitions

This "white space" between your scenes is of utmost importance when crafting your scene transitions. You have to decide at each of your transitions how much to show of the events that transpire between the scenes, if any.

In Chapter 4, I demonstrated how to connect the viewer emotionally with the hero by showing the hero's journey between the scenes after something big happens. I said that you can add an entire scene showing this emotional journey as he gets on a bus, train, airplane, or horse to travel to the next scene.

Conversely, there are instances where leaving out the hero's journey can convey emotion to the audience, if it is one of competence, expediency, or even depression. Let's say, for instance, your hero is a very detail-oriented detective. Using shock cuts between his scenes as he whisks from one place to another helps portray his efficiency. Or, what if your hero is a mailman on an established route which he travels every day? Cutting out his journey between houses, or even between days, can portray his boredom.

There's a really good example of this in the opening sequence of *Garden State*, in which the director, Zach Braff, cuts from Los Angeles to New York. The hero suddenly appears in the new place in the next scene. Braff indicates the long 6-hour flight with only sound effects — a jet plane's roar and air traffic control voices — during a brief fade-to-black. What does this lack of an on-screen journey do to portray the hero's emotion?

Garden State, *directed by Zach Braff.* © 2004 Fox Searchlight/Miramax. All rights reserved.

In this instance, the hero is in a complete daze, partially because he's on lots of antidepressants and because he is in shock over his mother's death. This shock cut represents his journey to the funeral and back to his home town. It lets us internalize his mental state — detached and not caring about anything. He pops from location to location seemingly without any journey. He is just there.

Throughout *Between the Scenes* one thing remains constant: showing less at a transition propels tension. Now we know it also provokes thought.

Deleted Scenes Revisited

The Gestalt adds another layer to the difficult decision of cutting out entire scenes. In earlier chapters we explored the rhythmic reasons to remove a scene, either because it slowed the pace or didn't harmonize with the moods of the surrounding scenes.

As weird as it sounds, deleting scenes can help the audience feel more connected to the material. Either it provokes their imaginations to fill in the missing events, or it keeps things clear and concise enough to understand the story easier, or both. Or, perhaps it keeps a question going until it is answered in a later scene.

As the old saying goes — less is more.

WAYS TO SHOW TIME MANIPULATION

When you cut large chunks of time out of your film, leaving a gap between scenes, you're left with a decision to make. Do you simply leave this gap as a shock cut, or do you try to stylize this shift in time to make it more palatable to the viewer? Depending on your skill, this process is either a Band-Aid or an art form.

The Cut

The most basic forms of ellipsis between two scenes are the *shock cut* (or *straight cut*) which simply remove unnecessary story information in the interim between two events. The resulting jolt in continuity prods the viewer to fully realize that time and space have changed.

Whether this jolt is effective is dependent on the intensity of the aesthetic differences between the two scenes. If the visual shift is abrupt enough, or the sound level changes significantly, the audience will understand the change in time.

The shock cut also makes use of binary oppositions (as outlined in Chapter 2) between Scene A and Scene B to cue the viewer as to how much time has passed, e.g., night to day, rain to sunshine, etc.

While the straight cut between scenes was thought to be too confusing in the early days of filmmaking, it is now considered standard. In your film, using simple shock cuts to bridge all of your scenes might be sufficient, but you probably want to expand further than this.

Dissolve

The *dissolve*, once used for every scene junction, is today saved for moments of emotional expression. The dissolve is a soft boundary that minimizes collision, slows the macro-rhythm, and evokes a peaceful and reflective mood through its fluidity. Dissolves are used to release tension, or to help the viewer let go of something emotionally.

It was once thought that the dissolve should be used to cover a longer time gap than the cut, so that, for instance, it could be used to demonstrate several months passing rather than a few hours. While this may still be rationalized, the ultimate decisive factor is an emotional one. You'll most likely want to use a dissolve during a rhythmic ebb to enable your audience to relax or take time to process an emotion.

"Dissolves can create tremendous romance and feeling because they're surreal, I suppose. You're making more of a painting instead of exposition, not just taking people from one place to another but creating a different mood or reality."

— EMILY PAINE, editor

Wipe and Iris

Other variations include the wipe, which serves in moments when the junction needs to keep the speed of a cut while retaining the fluid boundary of a dissolve. George Lucas is known for his use of wipes and irises in the *Star Wars* trilogies (1977–2005); by combining the screen composition of the connecting frames of Scenes A and B he creates a fluid motion for the eye to follow.

In the example shown, Obi Wan and Luke are walking toward the right, and they simultaneously fly in on a scooter from screen-left. Since the wipe and the characters both move toward the right, fluid motion is created. Note that the wipe itself is a soft boundary which essentially turns it into a moving dissolve.

Star Wars, directed by George Lucas. © 1977 Lucasfilm/Twentieth Century-Fox. All rights reserved.

An iris is another form of wipe that originates from within the center of the screen, or moves toward the center from the outer edges of the screen. In early uses of the iris, filmmakers darkened the edges of the screen to create a spotlight effect on the subject. While the iris is rarely used today (outside of *Star Wars*), it was once popular in the silent film era.

When using the wipe or iris, one must be very careful to match motion and eye movements from one shot to the next. This makes the transition appear seamless.

Black Fade

Fading to black is another common style which forms a sharp demarcation between events, effectively serving to halt the forward momentum in order to start fresh. The fade to black completely disconnects the two scenes, and it takes the viewer out of the story.

It renders any collision or linkage between Scene A and B useless, as they are no longer juxtaposed, deflating any connection between them (see Chapters 2 and 3). The black space becomes a new third scene stuck in between. It's the same as a curtain pull on stage. The exception, of course, is when sound or music is used through the black space to link the scenes.

Formal titles are often used in the black space to label the beginning of a new chapter, as was done in Barry Levinson's *Sphere* (1998).

THE SPACECRAFT

Sphere, directed by Barry Levinson. © 1998 Warner Bros. Pictures. All rights reserved.

Fading to black between scenes or sequences tends to work well in documentaries and the factual telling of information, if you're going for the dry, formal style. It doesn't work quite as well when emotion is involved. Overusing it in drama can cause fatigue. I've seen a lot of student films that overuse black space between scenes. It has the effect of taking viewers out of the story, and if you do this too much it makes the viewer want to stay out. We want to spend time escaping inside your story world, not constantly being awoken from our fantasy.

Movie trailers use the fade-to-black because they are showing you a truncated series of bursts. This flashy effect utilizes binary oppositions to make things pop on the screen — content versus no content. It works for advertising, it doesn't work as well for longer-form storytelling.

TRANSITIONAL EDITING SPEED

The speed of editing within a scene also affects the speed of editing between the scenes.

In editing, there's a thing called the *Axis of Frequency*, which goes along with the *Axis of Proximity* (see Chapter 5). Essentially you arrange your material along emotional lines by manipulating the closeness of the shots to the actor (wide shots vs. close) and manipulating the length of time that shots remain on the screen (fast vs. slow).

During tense moments you would probably use a fast frequency of shots, and probably shoot closer and tighter to the subject. During less tense moments you may trend toward

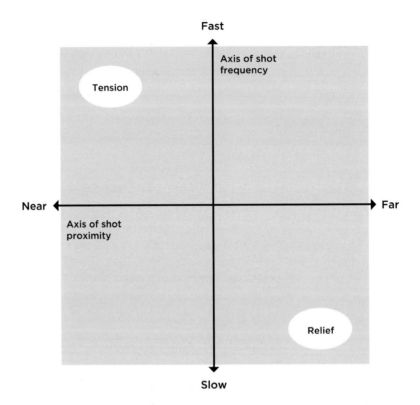

wider shots held longer on the screen. Though wide shots can be tense, too.

These axes are important to consider at the transitions because this is where shifts in time and place are the most dramatic. Go for the opposite. If you've been using tight and close edits during the scene, switch to long and wide edits at the transition.

Next, we look at some of the ways you can use fast or slow edited shots as transitions.

Time Collage

Collage in the art world involves assembling a lot of things in one small place. In film editing, *time collage* is a form of time manipulation serving the purpose of linking two scenes with a series of shortened mini-scenes, usually to summarize a series of events. It is also referred to as a montage.

Collage

Scene A		Scene B

Think about your script. You could use time collages between all of your scenes to show brief glimpses of the events that happened between your major events. But, remember Gestalt. You may want to leave this up to the viewer's imagination.

Time collage is especially good at demonstrating the passage of time on a person or object. Let's say your hero has been hurt, and you want to show how much time passes before someone comes to help. You could use collage like the Hughes Brothers did in *From Hell*. Just after a murder scene on the streets of London, we move from the murder in Scene A through a fluid time lapse. It utilizes the same camera frame as hours pass from night to morning, until Inspector Abberline (Johnny Depp) arrives the next morning.

This collage is composed of brief moments: the cloaked murderer running away from the body, a single policeman arriving hours later to discover the body, another policeman arriving later, and then a third and fourth policeman arriving later still. Soon, the single shot dissolves to random crowds beginning to arrive as sunlight flows in. All are connected by quick dissolves that create a fluid progression of events surrounding an unmoving corpse.

A single shot in the Hughes Brothers' From Hell *shows various people moving quickly around a motionless body as time passes.*

Time collage is not limited to story moments; it can sometimes take the form of photographs, as is the case in Robert Mulligan's *Same Time, Next Year* (1978), where the collages of historic events serve the dual purpose of painting cultural context, as well as indicating a passage of years. It becomes a kind of scenery (see Chapter 5) establishing the setting and the emotional context for the characters.

Probably the most common form of time collage you're used to seeing is the music video, in which a lyrical song is accompanied by fragmented narrative imagery. This is quite common in opening sequences, in which the song helps introduce a mood with fragmented scenery while the opening credits are displayed.

Aronofsky's Hip-Hop Montage

Time collage also enables the director to use multiple scene collisions in fast succession with sound effects, creating a hyperventilated rhythm. Edgar Wright's *Hot Fuzz* (2007) and Greg Marcks' *11:14* (2003) both use this between scene junctions.

This device, also known as the *hip-hop montage*, a term coined by writer/director Darren Aronofsky, utilizes a rapid burst of split-second images along with hyper-present sound effects, propelling the tension forward. It serves as a form of fast-forward where time is compressed in order to rush to the next big event.

The end of a scene with Alan Alda (A) triggers a montage of historic moments marking the passage of time. Same Time, Next Year. © 1978 Universal Pictures. All rights reserved.

(Continued on next page)

1977

B

Director Robert Mulligan's montage uses political, social, and cultural references to speed forward in time to an older Alan Alda (B). Same Time, Next Year.

Hot Fuzz hero Nicholas (Simon Pegg) is shown going through his routine as a policeman with a shock cut from his police car in Scene A to quick flashes:

1. His hand opening a locker

2. Making an entry in his log

3. Opening the locker again

4. Putting his hat on a shelf

Then Wright cuts immediately to Scene B at the police station. This example of the hip-hop montage lasts no more than a few seconds and is a prominent transitional style throughout the film. The shallow focus of the shots makes them seem to flow faster, as if it's a blur of action.

1

2

3

4

Reversing Time

In *11:14*, a film which follows multiple plot lines all coinciding at the time 11:14 p.m., Greg Marcks uses the hip-hop montage to rewind time as he switches from one plot line to another. In one example he moves from Scene A, cutting to white flashes of:

1. A bowling ball lies in the grass of a cemetery
2. Buzzy (Hilary Swank) and her boyfriend (Shawn Hatosy) in the back of a police car
3. A dead body lying on the highway
4. A view of the highway overpass before the body falls

He cuts then to the establishing shot of Scene B in a previous time. In the movie, we have just seen the scenes from which these shots are taken. They cue a reversal in chronology.

A hip-hop montage generates a feeling of manic, subjective presence on the screen instead of the traditional objective and reflective viewpoint of the slower collage. It's a lot like pressing fast-forward on a DVD.

Dividing the Screen

It's also not uncommon to demonstrate the passage of time by showing the hero doing multiple things simultaneously on a divided screen — each section of the screen is in a different time.

11:14, directed by Greg Marcks.

OTHER TIME STYLES

There are other devices by which writers can cue the audience that time has passed between scenes. Directors can also add these devices. Editors will have a tougher time adding them, but it can be done.

Two devices you can use are *temporal objects* and *ornamentals*. Temporal objects exist within the story world, and ornamentals are more like a picture frame or proscenium arch that wraps the story world with a dressing.

Temporal Objects

Temporal objects are simple. They are objects from within your story world having the sole purpose of indicating time has elapsed, such as clocks, calendars, burning candles, etc.

> *"The idea is to depict the ravage of time on an article that requires small spans of time to show marked changes in its appearance."*
>
> –DANIEL ARIJON, film scholar

Ornamentals

Ornamentals are extras added to a scene transition in order to make the presentation more overt. These ornamentals exist outside the story world and serve as a function of the narrator.

In director Jeremiah S. Chechik's holiday-themed comedy *Christmas Vacation* (1989), the passage of time at the ellipses is made overt by an Advent calendar with an unidentified hand reaching into the frame to uncover the next day. The calendar makes no appearance in the context of the story or the characters. It merely serves as thematic ornamentation to convey an aesthetic mood, similar to that of scenery.

On-screen graphics can help package your story into a specific theme. Director Jeff Schaffer's travel comedy *EuroTrip* (2004) utilizes on-screen graphics to indicate movement of characters across Europe. In keeping with the theme of traveling, *EuroTrip* opens with comic animations of in-flight passenger cards, and many of its subsequent scene transitions feature animated lines moving on a map, stylized with cutouts of cultural iconography of the locations visited. These ornamental graphics serve an aesthetic purpose: brightening the mood

A moving collage of tourist attractions in Jeff Schaffer's EuroTrip.

with a few laughs, accenting the omitted time of the journey, and providing mental maps for viewers unfamiliar with the geography (see Chapter 2).

Waitress (2007), directed by Adrienne Shelly, goes a step further in involving the hero in the transition, by way of a voice-over narration while we see her preparing various pies. At each transition, she demonstrates her newly invented flavors of pie which coincide with the mood she is feeling in the story.

WHEN NOT TO SHOW TIME PASSING

As always in the craft of scene transitions, going against conventional wisdom can prove effective as well. You may decide not to worry about time at all in your film. Perhaps your drama is so gripping that the audience isn't going to care whether time passed. Jumping and skipping through time without much differences in location and style can create the effect that time doesn't matter. It's clearly passing faster than screen-time, but for whatever reason the audience doesn't care.

In the climax sequence of *2001: A Space Odyssey* (1968), Stanley Kubrick creates one scene at one location spanning decades of time. Our hero arrives on location in a space suit. He sees his older self sitting at a desk. His older self looks back at his younger self. Soon the older self spots an even older self lying on a bed.

By not showing the passage of time, Kubrick makes the

2001: A Space Odyssey, directed by Stanley Kubrick.

viewer piece together what must have happened. I count this among the most brilliant transitions ever made.

GESTALT'S COUSIN

Now for the side effect of all this Gestalt. After you've cut so many things out, guilt sets in, and you begin to feel something really needs to be put back in. What if you've deleted a lot of material for good reasons — maybe the scene didn't flow rhythmically with the surrounding scenes, for example. But, you still feel the audience should see some of it.

In order to save it, you could add the material as a *flashback* or *flash-forward*. This is another form of time manipulation which, instead of creating gaps, actually fills in those gaps.

Flashbacks/forwards serve the function of connecting scenes through a subjective viewpoint, through the dream-like state of the mind. They can be inserted as triggers of memories from a character.

All of the same transition techniques that you've been learning throughout this book apply to flashbacks. When switching to a flashback, you still rely on binary oppositions (see Chapter 2) to demarcate the boundaries between reality and dreamworld, as well as utilizing hooks to link them.

Conversely, it is becoming more common for a flashback to be treated as part of the mixed time flow with no stylization whatsoever. This provokes the mind into making sense of the order of events. In the case of Darren Aronofsky's *The Fountain* (2006), flashbacks/forwards become a fluid part of the story to such an extent that the boundaries are ambiguous from shot to shot.

The greatest lesson to learn from this is — if you leave your audience to piece things together for themselves, as long as a story can be followed, they become more engaged in your tale.

GRAB YOUR SCRIPT

How have you handled the passage of time in your script? When looking at your transitions, here are some things to ask yourself:

- Which scenes can I leave out to keep the audience guessing?

- Which parts of deleted scenes can I put back in, as flashbacks or flash-forwards?

- Do I have a strategy toward how I will stylize my scene transitions? Which transitions will get straight cuts, which will get dissolves, and which will require a time collage?

- Is it obvious when time changes in my film?

CHAPTER NINE

CASE STUDY: RIDLEY SCOTT'S "GLADIATOR"

"I think one of the successes of 'Gladiator' is how we manage to turn on a dime the character from one thing to another where you believe he is one thing and he is something very different."

— RIDLEY SCOTT, director

Now that you've learned the art of scene transitions, you'll start seeing movies in a new way. Even better, you'll see your current script or film in a new way, hopefully strengthening your ability to connect emotionally with your audience.

In this chapter, we'll look at an example of a complex scene transition from *Gladiator* that uses all of the techniques mentioned in this book. This is to demonstrate that there is an endless variety of combinations you can use, and that you can use as many techniques as necessary in one transition. If there was any way to get your mind away from simple dissolves and wipes, this is it.

Ridley Scott has constructed a complex weave of scenery, transports, collages, flashbacks, binary oppositions — all in an emotionally charged journey connecting us to the feelings of the hero, Maximus.

THE LONGEST TRANSITION EVER

Gladiator is a film which follows the dramatic duel between two rivals, both wishing to take the reins of Ancient Rome. Our hero is Maximus and our villain is Commodus.

The scene transition that we're looking at is early in the film (00:40:00) at the ending of Act 1. As you'll recall, the transition at the end of this act is one of the major six transitions to focus on in any story (see Chapter 1).

Scene A is in the cold, misty Roman forest, where Maximus is about to be executed. He is kneeling on the ground, with a sword poking at the back of his neck, his executioner waiting for the order to be given.

Scene B is in the hot, sandy African province of Zucchabar. It is a small desert village whose citizens capture and train slaves to become gladiators. You'll note that already there is great contrast between these two locations.

Between these two scenes is an eight-minute scene transition, following Maximus on his journey from Scene A to Scene B. Along the way he escapes his captors, travels on horseback, goes home, finds his family slaughtered, is wounded, then captured and carried in a slave trader's wagon all the way to Africa. Not only is this journey emotional for Maximus, but it is portrayed in a way that lets us connect with Maximus. As he reacts to plot events we are pulled in. Scott could have easily turned it into a 30-second collage, just showing the important factual moments, but then it wouldn't be as emotional for the audience.

MAXIMUS ESCAPES EXECUTION - 00:00

Action: At the end of Scene A, Maximus turns the tables on his executors and escapes with one of their horses. He rides on horseback through the scenic hillsides of Ancient Rome.

Shot Selection: The opening moments of Maximus' flight from his enemies is a mix of extreme wide shots with close-ups of a horse's hooves galloping.

Transitional Styles:

- *Transport Scene* — This movement begins the transport scene showing the hero on his emotional journey through geography. We connect with the emotion of his escape, and his new sense of freedom upon avoiding execution (see Chapter 4).

- *Scenery* — Wide shots of the landscape provide relief from the tension of the forest he has escaped from (see Chapter 5).

- *Music* — The music kicks in late, in a silence-to-music configuration, allowing us to experience the emotional release of what has just happened (see Chapter 6).

- *Time Collage* — The entire movement is a collage. Each shot is a separate moment in time, presumably with missing time in between (see Chapter 8).

SLEEPING THROUGH THE NIGHT – 01:41

Action: A full moon is shown. Maximus is sitting by a camp fire. We hear his thoughts in voice-over.

Shot Selection: This sequence uses a combination of extreme wide shots with extreme close-ups on Maximus.

Transitional Styles:

- *Binary Oppositions* — This movement begins with a sudden cut from day to night, which also involves a change from moving to stillness. These opposites help demarcate this moment and demonstrate a passage of time (see Chapter 2).

- *Transport* — This continues the transport scene. He is still on his journey, reacting emotionally to the event of his escape (see Chapter 4).

- *Scenery* — The shot of the moon provides an ebb of relief. Since the actor is not in the shot, it gives us a break from him (see Chapter 5).

CROSSCUTTING TO FAMILY'S MURDER – 02:10

Action: Maximus rides on horseback continuing his journey. Suddenly he realizes that his family is in danger of being killed as well. He stops, turns his horse, and races toward home. Meanwhile, his family is slain.

Shot Selection: A continuation of extreme wides and closes. This movement crosscuts between Maximus and his family's murder.

Transitional Styles:

- *Crosscutting* — Clearly, the crosscutting here builds tension between the two events and creates the hope that Maximus will arrive in time to save his family (see Chapter 7).

- *Binary Oppositions* — Suddenly it's daytime from a previous scene of night (see Chapter 2).

- *Transport* — It essentially ends his journey of escape, and becomes a new journey as Maximus reacts to the idea that his family might be in danger. The audience connects with this shift of emphasis because we also can see what he doesn't see — that his family really is being murdered. We connect to his race to save them because we were allowed to follow his reaction and new journey through geography. We were also treated to a shift in context with this privileged knowledge (see Chapter 4).

- *Scenery* — There is a continuation of the scenery shots we've seen throughout this entire transition. Not only do they provide aesthetic relief from the cold, dreary scenes from the beginning of the film, but they also provide a sense of scale. He has such a long ride ahead of him, maybe not enough time to save his family. Also, the shots appear on the screen without him, giving us a sense of anticipation until we see him enter the frame (see Chapter 5).

THE BIG REACTION – 03:55

Action: Maximus sees that his family has been killed. He reacts by collapsing, burying them, and then falling asleep.

Shot Selection: A mix of wide (shallow focus), and close.

Transitional Styles:

- *Transport* — In Chapter 4, you learned that a character can react by standing still, especially if it contrasts with a lot of previous movement. Maximus reacts to seeing his family by freezing up and barely moving. He is now reacting to new plot intensity (see Chapter 4).

- *Time Collage* — Time has been cut out of this movement. We don't get to see him digging the holes or finding the flowers to place on top of the graves (see Chapter 8).

- *Binary Oppositions* — There is a cut to black at the end of this movement, giving the audience a jolt, and forcing us to look at what just happened in its entirety. This separates what follows from the previous shot (see Chapter 2).

CARRIED TO ZUCCHABAR – 05:27

"Gladiator is one of my favourite adventures because I really loved going into the world. I loved creating the world to the degree where you could almost smell it."

— RIDLEY SCOTT, director

Action: Maximus is being carried in a wagon over a vast distance from his home to Scene B, the final destination of his journey — the African province of Zucchabar.

Shot Selection: It begins with a black screen, followed by close-ups of Maximus intercut with his point of view looking up at his captors. This is intermixed with scenery shots and flash-forwards.

Transitional Styles:

- *Hip Hop Montage* — Quick flashes of scenery and other shots are used in order to paint the nightmarish nature of Maximus' mind (see Chapter 8).

- *Transport* — The long transport from Rome to Zucchabar continues on its last leg. This time, the hero's reaction shifts from the loss of his family to the reaction to his abduction as he slowly regains consciousness along the journey (see Chapter 4).

- *Scenery* — The widest scenery shot of the entire eight-minute sequence is placed here. It is a vast panning shot of the African desert. The sequence ends with another wide establishing shot of Scene B (see Chapter 5).

- *Flash-forward* — The use of flash-forwards inserts story information into the mix. They are stylized to demarcate them from the perceived reality (see Chapter 8).

Now that you've seen how complicated one scene transition can be, perhaps there's a transition in your film which could be expanded into something similar. It would be a key moment of change for your hero, as he travels from one event to the next.

As you can see, the world of transitions is at your fingertips!

All photos in this chapter are from Gladiator, *directed by Ridley Scott.*

CHAPTER TEN

TELEVISION VS. FEATURE FILM TRANSITIONS

"If you're playing the movie on a telephone, you'll never in a trillion years experience the film...
you'll be cheated."

— DAVID LYNCH, director, writer

Screen size matters. When you're making those decisions at the scene junctions as to whether to show the wide shot, the quick cuts, or the close-ups, the size of the final display screen makes a difference.

Display screens today range from the giant IMAX to the tiny iPhone screen. Experiencing the same styles of shot selection and editing speed feels much different on each. The close-up becomes intrusive on IMAX, and the long, picturesque scenery shot loses its glory on an iPhone.

The size of the final display screen has a massive impact on how a transition is viewed and experienced. Thus, it affects the choices you make at the transition as to whether the final screen is big or small. As a result, writers, directors, and editors must have in mind how their final product is going to be viewed. This decision is a complex one, since most films are seen in a variety of ways.

FILM AND TV DIFFERENCES

The obvious difference between film and TV is the venue. When you're in a theater, you're with a captive audience and have a shared experience. At home, you're more likely to have distractions and a lot more choices on other channels. If you don't like what's on, you can pop in a DVD or surf the Net. If you're with family and friends, you're more likely to talk back to the TV and provide commentary, something you wouldn't think of doing in the hush of a darkened cinema.

In television there is a drive to capture attention and keep it at every single point of the show — to prevent people from changing the channel and to grab people who just joined the show in progress. Since there are a lot of directors who migrate from television to feature film production, there is a tendency to forget the mediums are different. Feature films do not require this grabbing of full attention at every moment. Feature films are designed with space in which the audience can ponder.

Unfortunately, after the turn of the millennium, Hollywood is trending away from this as the marketplace moves toward DVDs and home viewing. One could venture to guess that the reason TV directors are being brought in to direct blockbusters is the notion that their TV style will be strong on DVD. The art of the feature is changing fast.

I recently had the rare opportunity to watch a 70mm theatrical screening of Stanley Kubrick's *2001: A Space Odyssey* at the Astor Theatre in Melbourne. Even though I had seen this film many times over the years on video and Hi-Def TV, this felt like I was seeing it for the first time. Always before it was slow and tedious, but this screening felt fast, ever present, and monumental.

It's not that we have short attention spans today and just aren't smart enough to handle slow films. It really is the screen size and the venue that play a role in how we perceive the pacing.

In the theater I was seeing the clarity and color depth of 70mm film. It was projected on a massive screen dominating the dark room. The crisp surround sound reached every seat within the classically designed hall. Sharing the experience with a packed house made this feel like a live event. We were sharing something amazing.

Watch the same film on video and it brings up feelings of "Ugh! Get on with it." The reason for this is simple.

Big things can hurt us. For very good reasons, humans have an instinctual sense that goes back millions of years to survival in the wild. If you're walking on an African savannah and you see a small lion cub, you may not be afraid. But when the mother lion shows up, a chill goes up your spine. Size matters. We get a thrill out of big things; giant trees in Yosemite, vast distances at the Grand Canyon. Humans are viscerally affected by giant size. Conversely, small things such as flies are just an annoyance.

Let's say your next film has a vast canyon view with a long, sweeping crane shot that tilts downward to show the menacing drop to the bottom. What will be the reaction when you show it to someone on their little phone screen? Nothing. They may appreciate the view intellectually, notice it has good production values and screen composition, but they won't feel it in their spine. Show the same view projected on a giant wall and they'll be mesmerized. They may even lose their balance for a second.

And let's not forget the actors. When an actor's face is projected on a big screen, you can see the nuances in their eyes, brief glimpses of emotion that you just wouldn't notice on a smaller screen.

The size of the final display screen instructs the choices you make along the Axes of Proximity and Frequency (see Chapters 5 and 8). You'll have a natural tendency to use less lingering wide shots when editing for a small screen. You'll also tend to show quicker edits because you know the viewer's attention will be briefer on a phone screen.

These differences have affected the styles for television and film for the last several decades. In the early days of television, the screens were very small and round. Camera shots tended to be closer in order to bring the actors closer to the screen, and thus more present in your living room. Cinema went the opposite way and used wider screens to capture panoramic views. For many decades, there were different styles for each medium.

Today things are changing, as home theater TV is becoming much closer to the cinema in terms of screen size and resolution. With the popularization of Hi-Def television, wide shots now have more power at home. At the same time, people are drifting toward Internet videos which are viewed on smaller screens (tablets, phones, laptops) which have replaced what TV used to be.

So what do you do as a filmmaker? If your final audience is going to be viewing on a wide variety of screen sizes, what choices do you make in the edit? You may choose to edit for the biggest screen it will be seen on, unless it's being produced exclusively for Internet streaming. Perhaps you may want to find a happy medium that takes both extremes into account. The good news is: When it comes to transitions, basic things like character movement through geography and location choices don't change, regardless of the screen size.

COMMERCIAL BREAKS

If you're writing, editing, or directing for TV, you may have to take commercial breaks into account. You first have to acknowledge that the viewer will have several five-minute breaks away from the story and may forget things. It is not uncommon for a character to summarize the plot throughout a TV script. This allows viewers' memories to catch up and informs new viewers just tuning in.

Second, your major emotional transitions don't necessarily have to fall at the end of each segment. If you plant them within a segment, you can follow your hero's reactions to new plot events and create a stronger bond with the audience. Save your end-of-segment plot revelations for the more minor twists. These will still keep the audience coming back after the commercial, but open up your bigger moments for more on-screen creativity.

Television borrows its use of commercial breaks from radio. Radio broadcasts throughout the 1900s included breaks for sponsors, as a way of providing free content for anyone with a radio that could pick up the reception. With the advent of cable and satellite programming, many channels still use commercial breaks as a major revenue stream.

Channels like HBO (Home Box Office) and Showtime create and broadcast series without commercials. These channels tend to blur the traditional formats in favor of a more uninterrupted cinematic style.

As of today, cinemas do not intervene with commercial breaks. If this ever changes, it will alter the rhythmic structure of feature films. No longer would filmmakers have to be clever in holding audience attention through an entire film. The cinematic art of the ebb and peak would fade.

MULTIPLE PLOTS

TV series, made-for-TV movies, soaps, and miniseries often use a cross-stitch weave of various plots. Many groups of characters follow their own stories, not always intersecting. This means that the contrast between worlds creates boundaries that help make sense of the separation.

Feature films have always done this, too, with their subplots, but increasingly there is a crop of multi-plot features springing up. Multiple-plot films have become an acceptable alternative to single-plot classical narratives. As a result, transitions have become an ever more essential art to master. More story lines mean more comparisons, more ways to use juxtaposition and opposition to propel these tellings forward in an emotional way.

It also means that the contemplation — that overall story puzzle — becomes even more important as a tool to paint emotional moods and environments for these story events as they intersect. (See chapters 4 and 5.)

THE FUTURE OF STORYTELLING

It is quite probable that within the next century, storytelling will migrate toward a more interactive and three-dimensional format. We will be able to immerse ourselves in fictional environments and interact with characters and events, either through virtual reality or holograms, or both. Gaming and cinema will continue to merge. The art of transitions in this future will also grow with it.

When a viewer is immersed in a world and surrounded by a panoramic environment, those shifts in scenery and time are going to be even more visceral than they are now on a flat portrait screen. Storytellers will have to know these principles and learn to adapt them, either to soothe the audience's senses at the time of transition, to disorient the audience, or to connect them emotionally with the characters as these characters react to plot events.

If these future formats ignore the art of transitions that have grown out of literature and theater for eons, I predict they will fail, because they won't connect with the participant on a storytelling level. They would become nothing more than 3-D gaming environments where participants experience a flat, emotionless checklist, disconnected from plot consequences and empathy for characters. This would be a shame.

I have analyzed transitions and their powerful storytelling possibilities for the first time in this book. Trends may change, but it is my hope that the art of transitions will continue to grow stronger, as more and more directors, writers, and editors take them seriously as storytelling devices.

CONCLUSION

Together we've journeyed through the murky, instinctual territory of scene transitions, and turned it into a clear and easily understandable art. With these new cinematic tools at your fingertips, you have the power to create vivid moments of emotion that move audiences. No longer will you have to struggle in fitting your scenes together.

Our journey of exploration doesn't end here. There is so much yet to discover about the space between the scenes. I've opened up the doors of possibility for you. Now all you have to do is walk through!

Safe travels.

GLOSSARY OF TRANSITION STYLES

- **Caboose Scene** – a transitional scene which has no dramatic ending. Instead of the traditional peak to a climax, the ending of this scene trails off to an ebb without any added plot. Commonly this is the last scene of the film.

- **Collage – Hip-hop Montage** – a quick selection of scene fragments, usually with a rhythmic or musical accompaniment in the soundtrack. Quickly summarizes a sequence of events.

- **Collision** – junction with a stark contrast between the aesthetics of the scenes. Sometimes multiple scenes are crosscut together from scene fragments.

- **Crosscutting** – two or more scenes are fragmented and mixed together in an alternating sequence, generating tension.

- **Cut** – the shortest form of junction, brings immediate shift in space and/or time.

- **Diegetic News Media** – news headlines from within the fictional story world: spinning newspaper headlines, TV and radio news reports, newsboys yelling "Extra! Extra!"

- **Dissolve** – extended junction which makes the junction aesthetically smooth over a graduated period of time.

- **Ellipses** – any junction which truncates or telescopes time in order to remove events in the story. Deleted material can provoke the viewer to think of what is missing.

- **Event Scene** – the most basic and common form of scene with a standard dramatic shape. A setting is staged, something happens, and the characters react. Placing two event scenes together creates a standard transition.

- **Flashback/Hyper-reality** – a junction which moves in or out of a subjective or dream state, often with a different color aesthetic or lens effects. This may also include found video footage contrasted against film.

- **In Medias Res Scene** – a transitional scene which has no beginning and no clear meaning. It is introduced by its sudden shock value of events *already in motion*, forcing the viewer to puzzle together a storyline.

- **Linkage** – a connective similarity between two scenes that fuses them together narratively at the junction.

- **Music** – provides relief or propels tension at the junction, expression of emotional moods, and provides orienting context to narrative objects.

- **Optical Effects** – includes wipes, iris ins/outs, page turns, animated maps.

- **Ornamental** – an object or graphical element at the junction which is separate from the story or character world, serving as a function of the narrator to generate a theme or mood.

- **Scenery** – provides "necessary relief" in the form of land-scapes, cityscapes in an objective wide shot, or portions of a locale from a more subjective viewpoint.

- **Sounds** – a junction is linked by sound effects, often serving as either punctuation, or as a sonic representation of the shift in time and space, e.g., a "whoosh."

- **Subplot Scene** – a transitional scene which follows sup-porting characters not connected directly to the main plot. It allows the audience to take a break from the main story, or find out information behind the hero's back.

- **Synchronicity Node** – the moment when multiple plot lines are linked together through an object, location, or encounter by random chance.

- **Temporal Objects** – a passage of time is marked by an object which visually represents the passage: clock, burning candles, sun rising, etc.

- **Titles and Captions** – the simplest and most formal way to describe a change in time and space is to print it onto the screen, often white text on a black background.

- **Transport Scene** – character reacts to plot event by mov-ing through geographic space, usually on a vehicle such as car, train, airplane, or on foot.

FILMOGRAPHY

Alien (1979), Dir. Ridley Scott.

Babel (2006), Dir. Alejandro González Iñárritu.

Christmas Vacation (1989), Dir. Jeremiah Chechick.

Crash (2004), Dir. Paul Haggis.

Elephant (2003), Dir. Gus Van Sant.

11:14 (2003), Dir. Greg Marcks.

EuroTrip (2004), Dir. Jeff Schaffer.

Face/Off (1997), Dir. John Woo.

The Fountain (2006), Dir. Darren Aronofsky.

From Hell (2002), Dir. Hughes Brothers.

The Fugitive (1993), Dir. Andrew Davis.

Garden State (2004), Dir. Zach Braff.

Gerry (2003), Dir. Gus Van Sant.

Gladiator (2000), Dir. Ridley Scott.

Good Will Hunting (1997), Dir. Gus Van Sant.

The Graduate (1967), Dir. Mike Nichols.

Hot Fuzz (2007), Dir. Edgar Wright.

Inside Man (2006), Dir. Spike Lee.

It's a Mad, Mad, Mad, Mad World (1963), Dir. Stanley Kramer.

Jaws (1975), Dir. Steven Spielberg.

Lifeboat (1944), Dir. Alfred Hitchcock.

Miller's Crossing (1990), Dir. Coen Brothers.

Mission to Mars (2000), Dir. Brian De Palma.

Offing David (2008), Dir. Jeffrey Michael Bays.

Phone Booth (2002), Dir. Joel Schumacher.

Psycho (1960), Dir. Alfred Hitchcock.

Requiem for a Dream (2000), Dir. Darren Aronofsky.

Rope (1948), Dir. Alfred Hitchcock.

Same Time, Next Year (1978), Dir. Robert Mulligan.

The Shining (1980), Dir. Stanley Kubrick.

Sphere (1998), Dir. Barry Levinson.

Star Wars trilogies (1977 – 2005), Dir. George Lucas.

Syriana (2005), Dir. Steven Gaghan.

Timecode (2000), Dir. Mike Figgis.

Titanic (1997), Dir. James Cameron.

2001: A Space Odyssey (1968), Dir. Stanley Kubrick.

Waitress (2007), Dir. Adrienne Shelly.

The Wizard of Oz (1939), Dir. Victor Fleming.

BIBLIOGRAPHY

Aumont, J 1979, *Montage Eisenstein*, Indiana UP, Bloomington.

Aumont, J; Bergala, A; Marie, M; Vernet, M (Eds) 1983, 'Montage,' in *Aesthetics of film*, University of Texas Press, Austin.

Arijon, D 1976, 'Film punctuation,' in *Grammar of the film language*, Los Angeles, Silman-James Press.

Aronofsky, D 2000, *Requiem for a Dream*, audio commentary, Artisan Entertainment.

Barthes, R 1977, *Image music text*, Fontana Paperbacks, London.

Berger, A 1997, *Narratives: in popular culture, media, and everyday life*, Thousand Oaks: Sage Publications.

Bordwell, D 1972, 'The idea of montage in Soviet art and film,' *Cinema Journal*, Vol. 11, No. 2, pp. 9–17.

Bordwell, D 1985, *Narration in the fiction film*, Methuen, London.

Bordwell, D 1993, *The cinema of Eisenstein*, Harvard University Press, Cambridge, Mass., pp. 120–190.

Bordwell, D 2006, *The way Hollywood tells it*, California UP, Berkeley.

Bordwell, D 2008, 'The hook: scene transitions in classical cinema' David Bordwell's Website on Cinema, http://www.davidbordwell.net/essays/hook.php.

Bordwell, D; Thompson, K 1991, *Film art: an introduction 8th Ed.*, New York, McGraw Hill.

Brooks, P 2001, 'Narrative desire,' *Narrative dynamics*, Ed. Richardson, Brian, Ohio State University Press, Columbus.

Chamberlin, C. J. 2006, 'Dziga Vertov: the idiot,' *Senses of Cinema*, sensesofcinema.com.

Chatman, S 1978, *Story and discourse: narrative structure in fiction and film*, Cornell University Press, New York.

Cohen, A 2001, 'Music as a source of emotion in a film,' *Music and emotion: theory and research*, Eds. Juslin, Patrick N. ; Sloboda, John A., Oxford University Press, New York, pp. 249–272.

Cohen, T 2005, *Hitchcock's cryptonomies: volume 2, war machines*, University of Minnesota Press, Minneapolis.

Cook, D 1975, 'Some structural approaches to cinema: a survey of models,' *Cinema Journal*, 14:3, p. 41–54.

Crittenden, R 1981, *Thames and Hudson manual of film editing*, London, Thames and Hudson.

Dmytryk, E 1984, *On film editing: an introduction to the art of film construction*, Focal Press, London & Boston.

Dundes, A 1997, 'Binary opposition in myth: the Propp/Levi-Strauss debate in retrospect ' *Western Folklore*, 56:1, p. 39.

Eisenstein, S 1945, (trans. 1987), *Nonindifferent nature*, New York, Cambridge UP.

Fabe, M 2004, *Closely watched films: an introduction to the art of narrative film technique*, Berkeley, University of California Press.

Ganti, K 2004, 'In conversation with Walter Murch ' *FilmSound. org*, Accessed 4 March 2011: http://filmsound.org/murch/interview-with-walter-murch.htm.

Godard, J 1972, *Godard on Godard: critical writings*, Eds. J Narboni and T Milne, Secker & Warburg, London.

Goldsmith, J 2006, 'Syriana Q&A,' *Creative Screenwriting Magazine*, podcast, Accessed 5 August 2010: http://creativescreenwritingmagazine.blogspot.com/2006/01/syriana-qa.html.

Gorbman, C 1987, 'Why music? The sound film and its spectator,' in *Unheard melodies*, Indiana University Press, Indianapolis, pp. 53–69.

Howard, R (2007, January 9), *USC School of Cinema Arts Series, iTunesU* [audio podcast], University of Southern California. Retrieved from iTunes.

IMDb: Internet Movie Database, http://www.imdb.com.

Iser, W 1978, *The act of reading: a theory of aesthetic response*, Johns Hopkins University Press, Baltimore, USA.

Kuhn, A 2005, 'Thresholds: film as film and the aesthetic experience,' *Screen*, vol 46, no 4, pp. 401–414.

Kuleshov, L 1929 (trans. 1974), *Art of cinema*, Berkeley, University of California Press.

LaBrutto, V 1991, *Selected takes: film editors on editing*, Praeger Publishers, New York.

Lefebvre, M 2006, *Landscape and film*, Routledge, New York.

Martin, A 2009, 'Beyond the fragments of cinephilia: towards a synthetic analysis,' in *Cinephilia in the age of digital reproduction*, eds. S Balcerzak and J Sperb, Wallflower Press, New York, pp. 30-50.

McKee, R 1997, *Story: substance, structure, and the principles of screenwriting*, Harper Collins, New York.

Murch, W 1992, *In the blink of an eye: a perspective on film editing*, AFTRS, Australia.

Oldham, G 1992, *First cut: conversations with film editors*, University of California Press, Los Angeles.

Ondaatje, M 2002, *The conversations: Walter Murch and the art of editing film*, Bloomsbury Publishing, London.

Oxford Dictionaries Online 2011, *Oxford University Press*, Canada, viewed 20 May 2011, http://oxforddictionaries.com/.

Pallasmaa, J 2001, *The architecture of image: existential space in cinema*, Rakennustieto, Helsinki.

Pearlman, K 2009, *Cutting rhythms*, Focal Press, Oxford.

Peters, L 2008, 'Private fears in public places: network narrative...,' *Synoptique 12: Melodrama*, http://www.synoptique.ca/core/articles/private_fears_in_public_places/

Smith, Greg 1999, 'Local emotions, global moods,' in *Passionate views: film, cognition, and emotion*, Eds. Carl Plantinga and Greg Smith, John Hopkins University Press, Baltimore and London, pp. 113–126.

Smith, J 1999, 'Movie music as moving music: emotion, cognition, and the film score,' in *Passionate Views: film, cognition, and emotion*, Eds. Carl Plantinga and Greg Smith, John Hopkins University Press, Baltimore and London, pp. 147–167.

Stam, R; Burgoyne, R; Flitterman-Lewis, S, 1992, *New vocabularies in film semiotics: structuralism, post-structuralism, and beyond*, Routledge, New York.

Sterritt, D 1998, *Jean-Luc Godard: interviews*, University of Mississippi Press, USA.

Tan, E 1996, 'The psychological affect structure of the feature film', in *Emotion and the structure of narrative film*, trans. Barbara Fasting, Lawrence Erlbaum Association, New Jersey, pp. 195–204.

Thomas-Jones, K 2008, *Aesthetics and film*, Continuum International Publishing Group, UK, pp. 124–127.

Tirard, L 2002, *Moviemakers' master class : private lessons from the world's foremost directors*, Faber and Faber, New York.

Truffaut, F 1986, *Hitchcock/Truffaut with the collaboration of Helen G. Scott*, Paladin, London.

Walsh, R 2001, 'Fabula and fictionality in narrative theory,' *Style*, vol 35, no 4, p. 572.

Wright, W 1975, *Six guns and society*, University of California Press, Los Angeles.

ABOUT THE AUTHOR

JEFFREY MICHAEL BAYS is a film scholar, director, and radio producer with a Master of Arts in Cinema Studies from La Trobe University, Melbourne, Australia, and a graduate of the Webster University School of Communications in St. Louis, Missouri.

Jeffrey is most widely known for his feature-length radio drama *Not From Space* (2003), heard throughout America on XM Satellite Radio (now SiriusXM). This production launched his reputation worldwide as a pioneer in Internet-based audio theater, for which he was awarded the Mark Time

Award and the Communicator Award of Excellence.

There is no stronger advocate for Alfred Hitchcock's film techniques. Jeffrey maintains the popular blog *How to Turn Your Boring Movie Into a Hitchcock Thriller*, and directed his own Hitchcock homage — the Australian suspense film *Offing David* (2008).

He was born and raised in Missouri, served as a Cadet Lieutenant Colonel in the Civil Air Patrol, and currently lives in Melbourne, Australia.

To contact the author, e-mail: info@borgus.com
or go to: www.borgus.com

CINEMATIC STORYTELLING
THE 100 MOST POWERFUL FILM CONVENTIONS EVERY FILMMAKER MUST KNOW

JENNIFER VAN SIJL

BEST SELLER

How do directors use screen direction to suggest conflict? How do screenwriters exploit film space to show change? How does editing style determine emotional response?

Many first-time writers and directors do not ask these questions. They forego the huge creative resource of the film medium, defaulting to dialog to tell their screen story. Yet most movies are carried by sound and picture. The industry's most successful writers and directors have mastered the cinematic conventions specific to the medium. They have harnessed non-dialog techniques to create some of the most cinematic moments in movie history.

This book is intended to help writers and directors more fully exploit the medium's inherent storytelling devices. It contains 100 non-dialog techniques that have been used by the industry's top writers and directors. From *Metropolis* and *Citizen Kane* to *Dead Man* and *Kill Bill*, the book illustrates — through 500 frame grabs and 75 script excerpts — how the inherent storytelling devices specific to film were exploited.

You will learn:
· How non-dialog film techniques can advance story.

· How master screenwriters exploit cinematic conventions to create powerful scenarios.

"Cinematic Storytelling scores a direct hit in terms of concise information and perfectly chosen visuals, and it also searches out... and finds... an emotional core that many books of this nature either miss or are afraid of."

— Kirsten Sheridan, director,
Disco Pigs; co-writer, *In America*

"Here is a uniquely fresh, accessible, and truly original contribution to the field. Jennifer van Sijl takes her readers in a wholly new direction, integrating aspects of screenwriting with all the film crafts in a way I've never before seen. It is essential reading not only for screenwriters but also for filmmakers of every stripe."

— Prof. Richard Walter,
UCLA screenwriting chairman

CINEMATIC STORYTELLING
THE 100 MOST POWERFUL FILM CONVENTIONS EVERY FILMMAKER MUST KNOW   JENNIFER VAN SIJLL

JENNIFER VAN SIJLL has taught film production, film history, and screenwriting. She is currently on the faculty at San Francisco State's Department of Cinema.

$24.95 | 230 PAGES | ORDER NUMBER 35RLS | ISBN: 9781932907056

FILM EDITING
GREAT CUTS EVERY FILMMAKER AND MOVIE LOVER MUST KNOW

GAEL CHANDLER

Film Editing: Great Cuts Every Filmmaker and Movie Lover Must Know makes the invisible art of editing visible by using nearly 600 frames from popular, recent films. The frames, accompanied by brisk descriptions, make it perfectly suited for quick study readers who like to 'gaze' rather than 'graze' and don't want to read a book. Written by an editor and the author of *Cut by Cut: Editing Your Film or Video*, it shows how editors can make or break a movie.

This one-of-a-kind book is your 'must have' cheat sheet to learning to make great cuts. Great for filmmakers, students or anyone who wants to see how the editor makes us believe. YouTubers, prepare yourselves to add juice to your creations.

"Those of us in the movie business often say that if we notice something, that means we didn't do a good job. Our job as filmmakers, is to do what we do as seamlessly as possible. Gael Chandler takes a microscope to those seams to show the subtleties and techniques used by seasoned professionals, using words and pictures that an average moviegoer or up-and-coming filmmaker can appreciate and experiment with. This dissection, together with quotes of working directors and editors, make Film Editing *a practical and aesthetic addition to any film buff, film student, or filmmaker's arsenal."*

— Victoria Rose Sampson, writer, director, film and sound editor; MPSE Award for Best Sound Editing: *Pirates of the Caribbean: Curse of the Black Pearl*, *Speed*, *Romancing the Stone*, *The River;* Grand prize winner for writing and directing, Harley-Davidson commercial contest short film, *Her Need for Speed*

"A comprehensive and easy-to-read description of the techniques editors use to seamlessly tell stories. The use of film frames clearly illustrates the editing concepts. A must-read for any film student, or anyone just interested in the art of editing."

— Nancy Morrison, A.C.E., editor, *Desperate Housewives*, *Starter Wife*, *Malcolm in the Middle*

GAEL CHANDLER has edited comedies, dramas, documentaries, features, corporate videos, and promos and cut on every type of medium: film, tape, and digital. Nominated twice for a Cable ACE award for editing a comedy series, she is a member of the Editors Peer Group of the Television Academy of Arts and Sciences and annually judges the Emmy and College TV awards.

$34.95 | 208 PAGES | ORDER NUMBER 129RLS | ISBN: 9781932907629

DIRECTING THE CAMERA
HOW PROFESSIONAL DIRECTORS USE A MOVING CAMERA TO ENERGIZE THEIR FILMS

GIL BETTMAN

The first half of this book is devoted to teaching a systemized approach that can be used to design the very best moving shot for any dialogue scene, no matter how complex or long. Bettman's "Five Task" approach enables the aspiring director to quickly grasp this difficult element of directorial craft. In the second half the reader is taught how to shoot action sequences using moving and static cameras and the gamut of lenses to achieve the magic trick essential to shooting action — making stunts that are highly controlled and neither violent nor dangerous look completely mind-blowing.

"*Directing the Camera* by Gil Bettman is by far the best book in print on the art of using a camera to tell a story. This book succeeds where most others on the topic fall short, because the author understands that a great movie is not a combination of cool shots, but rather a great story well told scene by scene."

— JoAnne Sellar, Academy Award–nominated Producer: *There Will Be Blood*.
Producer: *Inherent Vice, The Master, Magnolia, Punch-Drunk Love, Boogie Nights*

""Gil Bettman's great new book analyzes and defines the visual language of a number of groundbreaking directors and provides clear instruction on how to best emulate their craft. For anyone who wants to learn how to use the camera to tell a story as these directors do, it is a must-read.""

— William Teitler, Producer: *Rob the Mob, What Maisie Knew, Zathura, Empire Falls* (TV), *The Polar Express, How to Deal, Mr. Holland's Opus, Jumanji*. Executive Producer: *Tuck Everlasting, The Hurricane*

GIL BETTMAN is a director and a professor. He teaches at Chapman University in the Dodge College of Film and Media Arts. His book, First Time Director, made the Los Angeles Times bestseller list. He recently completed his fifth feature film, Go There Once, Be There Twice, a documentary recap of the life and times of rock star Sammy Hagar. Bettman has also directed numerous rock videos and multiple episodes of primetime television.

$32.95 | 232 PAGES | ORDER NUMBER 203RLS | ISBN: 9781615931668

MASTER SHOTS VOL 1 - 2ND ED.
100 ADVANCED CAMERA TECHNIQUES TO GET AN EXPENSIVE LOOK ON YOUR LOW-BUDGET MOVIE

CHRISTOPHER KENWORTHY

BEST SELLER

Master Shots gives filmmakers the techniques they need to execute complex, original shots on any budget. By using powerful master shots and well-executed moves, directors can develop a strong style and stand out from the crowd. Most low-budget movies look low-budget, because the director is forced to compromise at the last minute. *Master Shots* gives you so many powerful techniques that you'll be able to respond, even under pressure, and create knock-out shots. Even when the clock is ticking and the light is fading, the techniques in this book can rescue your film, and make every shot look like it cost a fortune.

Each technique is illustrated with samples from great feature films and computer-generated diagrams for absolute clarity.

"The camera is just a tool, and anyone who thinks making a movie is about knowing how to use a camera is destined to fail. In Master Shots, Christopher Kenworthy offers an excellent manual for using this tool to create images that arouse emotional impact and draw the viewer into the story. No matter what camera you're using, don't even think about turning it on until you've read this book!"

— Catherine Clinch, publisher
MomsDigitalWorld.com

"Though one needs to choose any addition to a film book library carefully, what with the current plethora of volumes on cinema, Master Shots is an essential addition to any worthwhile collection."

— Scott Essman, publisher,
Directed By magazine

CHRISTOPHER KENWORTHY has worked as a writer, director, and producer for the past ten years. He directed the feature film *The Sculptor*, which played to sold-out screenings in Australia and received strong reviews. Recent works include sketch comedy for the BBC's *Scallywagga*, a title sequence for National Geographic Channel, visual effects for 3D World, music videos for Pieces of Eight Records and Elefant Records, and an animated wall projection for The Blue Room Theatre in Perth, Australia. Kenworthy is the author of the best-selling *Master Shots*, two novels: *The Winter Inside* and *The Quality of Light*, and many short stories. Current projects include screenwriting, several directing assignments, and the development of additional *Master Shots* applications.

$26.95 | 362 PAGES | ORDER NUMBER 179RLS | ISBN: 9781615930876

MASTER SHOTS VOL 2
100 WAYS TO SHOOT GREAT DIALOGUE SCENES

CHRISTOPHER KENWORTHY

Building on the success of the best-selling *Master Shots*, this book goes much deeper, revealing the great directors' secrets for making the most of the visual during the usual static dialogue scene. A strong scene is determined from where you put the camera and how you position and direct your actors. This is especially true when shooting dialogue. The techniques in *Master Shots, Vol. 2* ensure that every plot point, every emotion, and every subtle meaning is communicated clearly.

This is the first book to show how important it is to shoot dialogue well. What's the point of opening your scene with a great camera move, if you then just shoot the actors like a couple of talking heads? *Master Shots, Vol. 2* gives you control of dialogue scenes, whether you're shooting two characters or a room filled with multiple conversations.

Using examples from well-known films, the book gives 100 techniques, lavishly illustrated with movie frame-grabs, and overhead diagrams, to show exactly what you need to get the required result. At all times, the techniques have been broken down to their core points, so they will work on a fully equipped Hollywood set, or with the most basic video camera.

"A terrific sequel to the first Master Shots. *If there's a cool way to move the camera, Kenworthy has explained it to us. I can't wait to get this book into my students' hands."*

> — John Badham, director, *Saturday Night Fever, WarGames*; author, *I'll Be in My Trailer*

"Master Shots, Vol 2 will inspire every filmmaker to think carefully about placement and movement of actors as seen through the camera lens. This book increases the reader's appreciation for the critical work of the cinematographer and the director as they speak the language of film through images."

> — Mary J. Schirmer, screenwriter, screenwriting instructor, *www.screenplayers.net*

CHRISTOPHER KENWORTHY has worked as a writer, director, and producer for the past ten years. He directed the feature film *The Sculptor*, which played to sold-out screenings in Australia and received strong reviews. Recent works include sketch comedy for the BBC's *Scallywagga*, a title sequence for National Geographic Channel, visual effects for 3D World, music videos for Pieces of Eight Records and Elefant Records, and an animated wall projection for The Blue Room Theatre in Perth, Australia. Kenworthy is the author of the best-selling *Master Shots*, two novels: *The Winter Inside* and *The Quality of Light*, and many short stories. Current projects include screenwriting, several directing assignments, and the development of additional *Master Shots* applications.

$26.95 | 240 PAGES | ORDER NUMBER 167RLS | ISBN: 9781615930555

24 HOURS | 1.800.833.5738 | WWW.MWP.COM

MASTER SHOTS VOL 3
THE DIRECTOR'S VISION
100 SETUPS, SCENES AND MOVES FOR YOUR BREAKTHROUGH MOVIE

CHRISTOPHER KENWORTHY

Master Shots has been one of the most successful filmmaking book series of all time. *Master Shots Vol 1, 2nd edition* and *Master Shots Vol 2* have generated cumulative sales of more than 60,000 copies and critical acclaim throughout the world. In this new volume, Kenworthy helps directors define their vision in every shot. This book provides the techniques to make a breakthrough film.

"Master Shots Vol 3 *offers fabulous insight into the purpose behind each shot. I'm so thankful for this book — it's my new secret weapon!*"
— Trevor Mayes, Screenwriter/Director

"*Finally! Someone has had the cleverness, initiative, and imagination to set down on paper a film language that has been passed down and amalgamated only by word of mouth since the days of Méliès and D. W. Griffith. Like Dr. Johnson's Dictionary of the English Language,* Christopher Kenworthy's Master Shots *series seeks to make tangible and permanent what otherwise might be gone with the wind.*"
— John Badham, Director, *Saturday Night Fever, WarGames, Short Circuit*; Author, *I'll Be in My Trailer* and *John Badham on Directing*; Professor of Media Arts, The Dodge School, Chapman University

"*A fascinating look at amazingly simple ways to use the camera, making this an essential read for anyone looking to hone the craft of visual storytelling.*"
— Erin Corrado, www.onemoviefiveviews.com

CHRISTOPHER KENWORTHY is the creator of a new series of Master Shots e-books (with HD video and audio) including *Master Shots: Action, Master Shots: Suspense,* and *Master Shots: Story.* He's the author of the best-selling *Master Shots Vols 1* and 2, with *Master Shots Vol 3: The Director's Vision* released in 2013.

$26.95 | 238 PAGES | ORDER NUMBER 196RLS | ISBN: 9781615931545

SETTING UP YOUR SCENES
THE INNER WORKINGS OF GREAT FILMS

RICHARD D. PEPPERMAN

Every great filmmaker has films which inspired him or her to greater and greater heights. Here, for the first time, is an awe-inspiring guide that takes you into the inner workings of classic scenes, revealing the aspects that make them great and the reasons they have served as inspirations.

An invaluable resource for screenwriter, cinematographer, actor, director, and editor, Pepperman's book uses examples from six decades of international films to illustrate what happens when story, character, dialogue, text, subtext, and set-ups come together to create cinematic magic.

With over 400 photos of selected movie clips laid out beautifully in a widescreen format, this book shows you how to emulate the masters and achieve your dreams.

"Setting Up Your Scenes *is both visually stunning and very useful for students of cinema. Its design, layout, and content make the book unique and irresistible.*"
    – Amresh Sinha, New York University/The School of Visual Arts

"*Pepperman has written a book which should form the basis for an intelligent discussion about the basic building blocks of great scenes across a wide variety of films. Armed with the information in this book, teachers, students, filmmakers, and film lovers can begin to understand how good editing and scene construction can bring out the best storytelling to create a better film.*"
    – Norman Hollyn, Associate Professor and Editing Track Head, School of Cinema-Television at the University of Southern California

"*Pepperman dissects some very infamous scenes from some very famous movies — providing us with the most breathtaking black and white stills — in order to highlight the importance of the interplay between dialogue, subtext, and shot selection in great filmmaking.*"
    – Lily Sadri, Writer, Screenwriter, *Fixing Fairchild*, Contributor to *www.absolutewrite.com*

RICHARD D. PEPPERMAN has been a film editor for more than 40 years and a teacher for more than 30. He is also the author of *The Eye Is Quicker* and *Film School*.

$24.95 | 245 PAGES | ORDER # 42RLS | ISBN: 1932907084

THE MYTH OF MWP

In a dark time, a light bringer came along, leading the curious and the frustrated to clarity and empowerment. It took the well-guarded secrets out of the hands of the few and made them available to all. It spread a spirit of openness and creative freedom, and built a storehouse of knowledge dedicated to the betterment of the arts.

The essence of the Michael Wiese Productions (MWP) is empowering people who have the burning desire to express themselves creatively. We help them realize their dreams by putting the tools in their hands. We demystify the sometimes secretive worlds of screenwriting, directing, acting, producing, film financing, and other media crafts.

By doing so, we hope to bring forth a realization of 'conscious media' which we define as being positively charged, emphasizing hope and affirming positive values like trust, cooperation, self-empowerment, freedom, and love. Grounded in the deep roots of myth, it aims to be healing both for those who make the art and those who encounter it. It hopes to be transformative for people, opening doors to new possibilities and pulling back veils to reveal hidden worlds.

MWP has built a storehouse of knowledge unequaled in the world, for no other publisher has so many titles on the media arts. Please visit www.mwp.com where you will find many free resources and a 25% discount on our books. Sign up and become part of the wider creative community!

Onward and upward,

Michael Wiese
Publisher/Filmmaker